MW01621162

"An inspirational business novel, Echoes Across the Tracks, will grab your attention from the very first scene and carry you from New Orleans to Chicago aboard a train abounding in success principles. "Echoes" is a refreshing approach that doesn't include workbooks or chapter summaries but rather gives the reader plenty of life & business lessons to reflect on. I can highly recommend it."

Gino Wickman, author of *Traction* and *Shine*, Creator of EOS

--- ### ---

"The best stories draw us in, entertain us, and spark transformation. Dave Moravec does all three in Echoes Across the Tracks. Don't buy a copy of this book; buy a dozen for all your friends."

Phil Callaway, radio host and bestselling author of *Laughing Matters*

--- ### ---

"Amazing! First-time author and long-time business pro Dave Moravec knocked it out of the park. If you are looking for a creative novel full of business and life lessons, you can't go wrong with Echoes Across the Tracks.

Dave Kerpen, NY Times Bestselling author of *Get Over Yourself*

--- ### ---

"Echoes Across the Tracks took me on a journey of discovery that enlightened me with business principles along the way. I felt like I was on the train, learning alongside Charlie."

Randy Wheeler, Maxwell Leadership Executive Program Leader and Faculty, author of Build, Engage, Lead: Mastering the 5 Keys to Effective Team Development

"In a serendipitous blend of nostalgia and expertise, my childhood love for trains harmonizes with my medical roots in Chicago, adding a personal touch to this enchanting tale. Dave, the master storyteller, seamlessly weaves his vast business experience into a spellbinding narrative set against the backdrop of a train ride. The characters and their interactions sparkle not just as pearls of business wisdom but as beacons of life's profound lessons.

As a curious physician, I traded my stethoscope for a ticket to a journey spanning generations, feeling like a fellow passenger awaiting Charlie's next encounter. This book isn't just a read; it's an immersive voyage inviting all to explore the transformative power of storytelling. So, grab your ticket and prepare for a ride that transcends time and space, promising enlightenment and self-discovery at every stop. All aboard! "

Abhinav Singh MD, MPH, FAASM, Physician and Medical Director of the Indiana Sleep Center, and author of *Sleep to Heal*

--- ### ---

"What an enjoyable read! Echoes Across the Tracks – Life Lessons Through Unexpected Connections guided me through the absolute joy of relaxing when plans unexpectedly change, embracing opportunities to begin new friendships, and seeing the potential magic in every situation. And it's filled with life and business lessons presented in a fun, imaginative, and useful way. Nice job, Dave Moravec! Nice job!"

Jeff C. West, award-winning coauthor, with Bob Burg, of *Streetwise to Saleswise: Become ObjectionProof™ and Beat the Sales Blues*

--- ### ---

"The book is a tale and is lots of fun to read. The life and business lessons are the bonus – unexpected *and* great!"

Harlan Geiser, Certified EOS Implementer® at EOS Worldwide

A special word from Dave Adkisson, Chamber of Commerce Leader and author of Horseshoes vs. Chess: A Practical Guide for Chamber Leaders

"Dave Moravec's book Echoes Across the Tracks spoke to me in a very personal way. As a former chamber of commerce CEO and former mayor of my hometown, I'm now retired and find myself reflecting on my circuitous, unplanned, but extremely rewarding career. I think of specific conversations from decades ago that seemed unremarkable at the time but, in retrospect, proved to be profound pivot points in my career. I can remember where I was sitting in my college cafeteria more than fifty years ago and a chance conversation that completely redirected my career trajectory. Such recollections, when pieced together, have allowed me to "map my career backward" through at least a dozen conversations that directly shaped my career and my life's work. Dave has captured the spirit of that serendipity in his Echoes, and I recommend it highly to anyone who is open to unexpected opportunities."

Echoes Across the Tracks

Life Lessons Through Unexpected Connections

David C. Moravec

2024

First Edition Design Publishing
Sarasota, Florida USA

Echoes Across the Tracks – Life Lessons Through Unexpected Connections

ISBN 978-1506-911-86-1 CL
ISBN 978-1506-911-87-8 PBK
ISBN 978-1506-911-88-5 EBK

LCCN 2024906704

April 2024

Published and Distributed by
First Edition Design Publishing, Inc.
P.O. Box 17646, Sarasota, FL 34276-3217
www.firsteditiondesignpublishing.com

Editor – Nancy Robjohns
Inside Illustrations – Renaldi Budiman
Cover Design – Anna Sophia

Disclosure - Amtrak, officially called The National Railroad Passenger Corporation, is a corporation that was chartered by the U.S. government in 1970 (operation began May 1, 1971). The federal government owns the majority of the stock (source), but despite this, Amtrak is classified as an independent agency. Amtrak has a Board of Directors that is appointed by the President of the United States, as well as a CEO and President. Additionally, Amtrak gets funding from multiple states and the federal government. This book uses the term "Amtrak" as it is the means of transportation in the narrative. The author and publisher recognize that Amtrak is a trademark and that the narrative in this book does not compromise the trademark in any way.

Any additional references in this fictional novel to products or services that would otherwise have registered marks (Twizzlers, Hyatt Regency, Honeywell, Subway, or others not named here) are purely to add a layer of verisimilitude and realism to the book. The use of Zig Ziglar's name and Miller's Pub Restaurant in Chicago has been approved by the authorizing parties.

Dedicated to those friends and family members who went before me—some too soon, some in old age—all as God intended. Gary, I'm looking forward to hearing another story from you someday.

Table of Contents

ACKNOWLEDGMENTS

I have heard it said that it is an author's first book that brings them their most joy; that is the case with me, but of course I don't have anything else to compare it to…just yet anyway. This book could not have happened without the help of my first reader, life partner and dedicated wife. Patti has given the book life and character through the love and joy she brings to me and to the world every single day with her kind words and smile. Thanks for saying yes to all of it.

I have been dedicated to the writing process as I have to sound business principles for over forty years. The difference today is that in authoring a book, I didn't know what I didn't know. As a life-long learner, I have a love for books, but now I have an ever-greater appreciation for those that have written them. A special thanks goes to the many publishing professionals that gave me guidance and directed me without personal gain, those who are truly givers and not takers in the industry; you know who you are. Believing that "people don't care how much you know, until they know how much you care" has been a central theme over the last several months, but at the heart of my approach throughout my life. A special thanks to Evan, who is a dedicated writer. You helped me get the beginning of the story right. Thank you!

My editorial rock, Nancy Robjohns, picked at the choices that I made, which challenged me to be a better writer and gave me pause to consider options that I would not have otherwise made. In the end, those choices made this book a much more polished piece while holding true to my goal of making it a fun page-turner. The cover design by Anna (South Africa) and inside illustrations by Renaldi (Indonesia) added to the creative juices during my editing process. Many thanks to those who weighed in on the art direction through an amazing process called CrowdSpring, whose founder is based in the Chicago area.

The cadre of business colleagues and friends who served as my initial peer readers, I can't thank them enough for giving of their time, especially during the holidays, to help guide Charlie's character development. I could have chosen so many others, but God put Keith, David, Randy, Janet, Ryna, Ron, Troy, Matt, Carrie, Karen, Quinn, and two very special Jeffs in my life for a reason, and I can't thank each of you enough for everything.

Harlan and Beth were left off of the list above because of a special relationship that I have with both of them. Harlan has been a longtime mentor, teacher, and friend who believed in me when many others did not. Harlan represents the quintessential "unexpected connection" in my book, and I am so thankful that God connected the two of us over 20 years ago. Beth is my current office administrator and now a lifelong friend. She and so many other supportive business colleagues, thought of me as "Just Dave" and appreciated my approach to leadership; each of you have a special place in my heart because you always made me look better because you forced me to look in the mirror.

Becoming a leader in the chamber of commerce industry doesn't come without the help of others along the way, especially as a late-in-life career pivot. Dave Adkisson, Josh, Isaac, Frank, Cindy, and other chamber leaders have given themselves to help me learn and apply sound business principles.

I have been blessed by a community that has embraced me in Colerain over the last four years, a board of directors and chairs like Susan and David who continue to support every step of my journey. Without the support of my local community here in Cincinnati as well as those in Bloomington-Normal and suburban Chicago in my past, my journey would have had far fewer success stories.

Finally, I have said that you don't get to pick your parents or your children; in most cases, that is. We really don't get to pick any of our family, for that matter. However, we can choose to live with them, learn from them, and love them unconditionally, regardless of age. I am so thankful for every family member living and who has passed on. I look forward to the next conversation with each of you, whether that is here on earth or at some point in the future in heaven. Thanks so much to those friends and family who love me for who I am.

Foreword

By Tom Ziglar

Dave Moravec is a storyteller—and a good one. Echoes Across the Tracks is a light and enjoyable read, replete with timeless lessons in grace and wisdom that carry from generation to generation. It is always great to learn from an author who lives such standards in his personal and business life. It's equally obvious he is serious about imbuing them in the generations following.

Interesting characters carry the many messages of eternal values Dave shares, while the setting he presents contributes to the overall pleasure of the reader's involvement in the story. He makes great use of questions, and how they contribute to meaningful conversations and can result in lasting interpersonal relationships.

Echoes Across the Tracks can be most valuable in teaching, exhibiting, and stressing the importance of living life on purpose...the purpose of enhancing one's own life as well as enabling and guiding others to build and experience solid personal and business principles and practices that ultimately result in better individual lives as well as more hopeful -- and helpful -- community. Virtually any age and any walk of life will benefit from exposure to this message. I know you will enjoy this book as it combines stories of the deepest grace and the highest standards.

Tom Ziglar
CEO of Ziglar Inc.

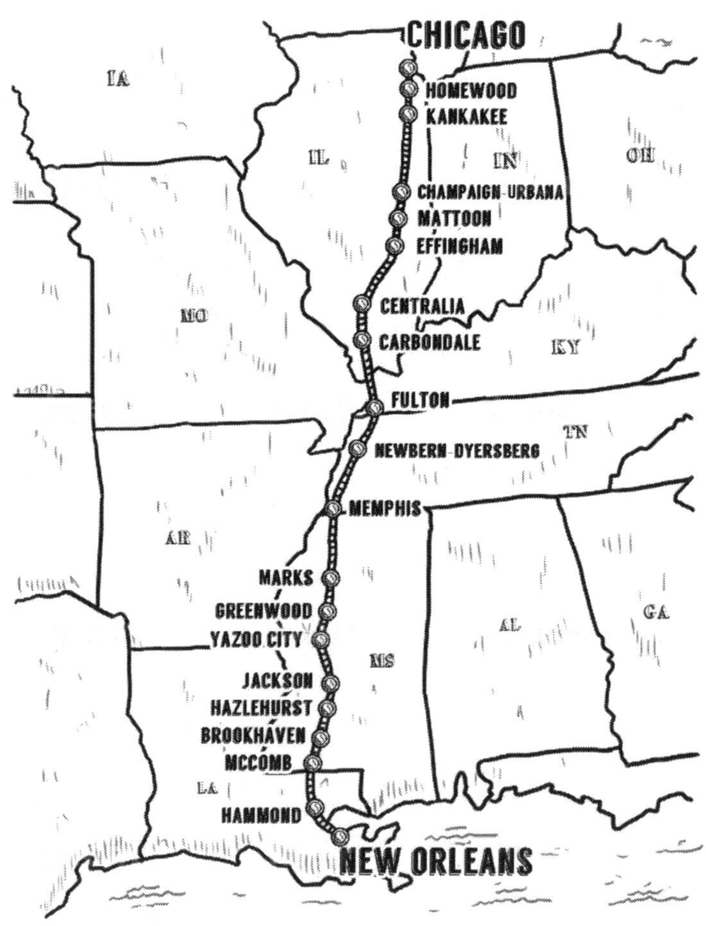

CHICAGO
HOMEWOOD
KANKAKEE
CHAMPAIGN-URBANA
MATTOON
EFFINGHAM
CENTRALIA
CARBONDALE
FULTON
NEWBERN-DYERSBERG
MEMPHIS
MARKS
GREENWOOD
YAZOO CITY
JACKSON
HAZLEHURST
BROOKHAVEN
MCCOMB
HAMMOND
NEW ORLEANS
IA
IL
IN
OH
MO
KY
TN
AR
MS
AL
GA
LA

CHAPTER 1

Change of Plans

Charlie's cab came to a stop in front of the New Orleans Union Passenger Terminal on this hot and humid late June afternoon. Steamy days in the deep south were commonplace; this one just happened to include a chance meeting and travel pivot, both of which Charlie often embraced.

"Mr. Charlie, we are here at the train station. Can I help you with your bags?

Charlie saw the price on the meter and couldn't believe it was only $19.00; it felt like an hour since leaving the convention center. "Aura, I have to hurry to catch the train. Thank you for the lift and for sharing your amazing story! We'll have to see how the train trip to Chicago works out, but thanks for the suggestion."

Charlie graciously handed the cabbie a $100 bill and suggested that he have a good dinner that evening. The two parted ways with a handshake that came to an embrace. Aura pulled Charlie close to his body and said, "You enjoy that train ride, Mr. Charlie. I will do as you suggest and have a good ol' fashioned cajon seafood dinner tonight. Thank you for allowing me to drive you."

Despite his need to catch the train, Charlie paused to watch Aura drive away before starting his walk to the station. The two waved at one another as if they had been friends forever. Both smiled as they went in different directions. Charlie noted the number of Aura's cab, 1978. He knew from their conversation that this was the year Aura came to the United States. Charlie would soon discover how a cab ride and echoes across the tracks can change the course of one's life.

--- ### ---

An hour earlier, Charlie had been running late for his flight to Chicago after his final session at the New Orleans Convention Center. After four days of steady sales following each leadership conference session he taught, only a few people stopped by his table. He had been invited back to this particular leadership conference for the third year in a row. This year was different because he could promote his most recently published book, *Modern Sales Methods and Leadership – Lessons from 1914 Applied Today.*

After rushing to box up the remaining copies of his book, Charlie signed the necessary paperwork at the convention center's shipping counter and let them take care of the rest of the details in getting the final partial case back to his home in Cincinnati. He had started the week with four cases of books; he was glad that he wasn't shipping home four cases. As he walked away from the counter, needing a ride to Louis Armstrong Airport. *I'll just catch the first cab outside and not look at the cost,* he thought to himself.

By this point, Charlie figured he could check on his flight from the cab to calm his adrenaline. His heart always raced when it came to being late to an airport.

Grabbing his rolling bag and briefcase, Charlie made his way through the vast hallways toward the cabstand, passing all the specialty shops in the convention concourse. His eyes glanced at the shop windows as he considered purchasing a gift for his wife, Rita. He didn't have time to be selective, so he kept walking. With far fewer attendees at the international sales conference on its last day, the halls seemed barren by convention center standards.

Getting to the cab stand and finding no people waiting, Charlie grabbed the first cab available.

"Where to?" the cab driver inquired as Charlie tossed his two cases into the back seat, not waiting for the cabby to open the trunk.

"The airport, please, and hurry!" Charlie understood the importance of being friendly to get the best cab service. After all, the guy could take the long route or end up charging him extra for the trip, which wouldn't help get him there any sooner. The sweat in his armpits was noticeable to him through the cotton

Oxford shirt and sports coat, so he whipped off his jacket before climbing in and shutting the cab door.

A dense fog engulfed the otherwise steamy city; visibility across New Orleans was like pea soup. As the cab driver navigated the narrow streets to the interstate, Charlie tried to pull up his flight; he had already checked in the night before. As the cab entered the on-ramp, an email notification came through Charlie's cell phone titled FLIGHT CANCELLATION NOTICE. Charlie's heart sank as he shook his head.

"Crap!" he mumbled under his breath, but loud enough that the cab driver heard him. Looking up at the cabby's rearview mirror, Charlie could see the driver's eyes fixed on him.

"Trouble, Boss?" Charlie noticed that the cabby had an accent of some kind.

Replying in a huff, "I think so; it looks like my flight to Chicago has been canceled."

"You still want to go to the airport? My name is Aura, and I can take you wherever you want to go."

"Yes, I'll have to check on other flight options and see what the problem is." Charlie had to be in Chicago by Thursday for a client meeting and another book signing that evening, but it was only Tuesday. His lunch with Sarge and his other high school buddies was on Friday afternoon, so he should be still okay despite the delay. "There are plenty of flights to O'Hare, and Midway is an option. Surely, I can get on one of them, right, Aura?"

"Yes sir, plenty of planes," Aura replied as he glanced in the rearview mirror at Charlie. "Would you consider riding the train instead? The train station is right over there," he said pointing toward the passenger side of the cab.

"No, Aura, I hadn't given it any thought at all," Charlie responded. "Heck, I don't even know how long a train ride would take from here to Chicago. Why did you bring up the train?"

Aura had a look in his eyes that suggested there was a story behind his recommendation. Needing to keep his eyes on the road in the fog, Aura continued, "The last plane I took brought me to Chicago in 1978. I was just 18 years old. Back in Africa, we rode the train or bus or took a car everywhere we went. I never flew on a plane before and never will again," Aura said with a misty tone to his voice. "I was escaping the terror in my country and got a flight to the U.S. in desperation. Chicago was too cold for my Ugandan body, and I found New Orleans as my final home."

He continued, "The Amin army killed my papa, and my brother also. None of us wanted to join the fight." Aura stopped the story abruptly. Contemplating the memory, he then continued, "I was in Chicago for a week, and the cold did not suit me because I was used to warm and even hot weather coming from East Africa. A wise man in Chicago told me to look into California, Texas, Florida, and New Orleans. I had what I brought with me in a pack and decided to take the train here. It took less than one day, and I had a new beginning."

Charlie opened another browser on his phone, *Train Schedule New Orleans to Chicago,* he typed as the cab headed on I-10 toward the airport.

"Aura, I like your idea, it could be a nice change of pace for me, and I'm not in as much of a hurry as I thought I was. Please take me back to the train station instead." Charlie had made a quick decision based on Aura's suggestion, but on such short notice, the App showed that no sleeping cars were available. At 70 years old, Charlie could sleep sitting up anywhere for a couple of hours. "The train leaves at 2:45 pm, so I should have time to make it if you take me there directly."

"Ok, you're the boss." As he continued, Charlie noticed Aura's eyes lit up in the rearview mirror again. "I met many people on that first train ride back then. Many people onboard looked at me funny. I am so dark-skinned, and back then, my accent was harder to understand. I spoke English, but I had to repeat everything I said. I speak much better now, don't you think?"

"Yes, Aura, your English is quite good now," Charlie agreed. "Are you married? Have a family here in New Orleans?"

Charlie had always been curious in conversations, inquiring about things that perhaps other strangers wouldn't. He learned that most people liked talking about their lives and telling their own stories. Charlie was an attentive listener, which allowed people to open up to him.

"My wife died in 2010, and I took to driving a cab after retiring from the shipyard here in N'awlins." Aura had changed his accent slightly to have a French Quarter tone about it. "My son moved to California after his mom died. He's an engineer with Honeywell and has two children of his own. He comes home once a year, but I haven't gone to see him. Don't wanna fly."

"Was the plane ride so bad leaving your home country?" Charlie asked inquisitively.

"Mr. Charlie, the things I saw over there were so bad that I can't even talk about them. I was on that plane to Chicago and only slept a few hours on my layover in Amsterdam. It was the worst 30 hours I had ever spent; I worried about the family I left behind and was nervous about what was ahead for my life. I didn't talk to anyone. Once I got to Chicago, I was so thankful to be in the United States but was still afraid of what was ahead for me — the unknown, that is. The train ride here to N'awlins was calming for me."

"But life turned out okay for you, right?" Charlie was more concerned about Aura's family today than his distant past. He knew that this was simply a brief conversation on the way to the airport; that was it.

"Yes, it did. I have had a very blessed life. The thought of an airplane trip just reminds me too much of my early life and family back in Africa. Do you have family, Mr. Charlie?

"I do, Aura. I am also blessed beyond measure. I am married; we have five adult children and seven grandchildren. Very blessed indeed," Charlie said. "Thank you for sharing your story with me, Aura. I have to run to catch the train. Thank you for the lift and for sharing your journey with me!"

Charlie walked into the station with his QR code boarding pass now saved to his phone. Technology advancements saved folks from going to a ticket booth, paying for, and getting a printed ticket. It likely eliminated some jobs but certainly made it more convenient for passengers.

Having not been in a train station for a couple of years, Charlie looked around and marveled at how many people were at the Union Terminal on a Tuesday afternoon. He admired the beautiful murals on the wall, which reminded him of all the murals across his home city of Cincinnati.

The customer service counter attendant alerted Charlie that the train to Chicago was already running late due to a fueling delay. This relaxed him enough that he no longer felt rushed.

He saw a sign for the Magnolia Room and figured that was an excellent place to grab lunch; however, when Charlie arrived, he was disappointed by the sign on the door: *Sleeping Car Passengers Only. See Ticket Agent for Access.* Charlie understood that he likely wasn't welcome in this area as he peeked through the glass. Unless he wanted to venture back out into the heat of the day, the only place to get something to eat was the Subway shop in the station.

By this point, his stomach was talking to him – almost anything would do. After grabbing a roasted turkey sandwich, Charlie found a seat in the waiting area and placed his bags by his side; eating a sandwich on his lap was common.

Shortly after sitting down, a young man sat down next to him. Charlie continued to eat his sandwich and glanced over at the young man. As people often do, Charlie created a scenario in his head about the young, professionally dressed African American man and where he was going. Traveling light, he only had a small duffle bag with wireless white earbuds keeping his attention. His eyes were closed but opened occasionally to check out the rest of the people in the station.

The young man caught Charlie's eye as he popped out his earbuds. "Can I help you? You were staring at me." Charlie seemed surprised at his abruptness. "I'm sorry, you just reminded me of a man that I just met in New Orleans, but he is much older than you are."

"Nope, not him," he replied jokingly. He leaned across in a friendly manner, extending his hand to Charlie. "My name's Jackson."

"Jackson, as in Jackson, Mississippi?" Charlie was certain that was going to be the answer.

"Yes, sir, Jackson Lewis. Yes, I was born there," the man offered. "Been looking for work anywhere I could and hoped that New Orleans might be the ticket. I interviewed for a job here yesterday and hope to hear back from them sometime soon. Been out of work for three months, and my family ain't got much back in Jackson. My wife and son are counting on me. Heading home, as a matter of fact."

"What kind of job were you interviewing for?" Charlie's gentle disposition and wide honest smile let Jackson know that he was in a safe place to answer. Charlie seemed to have an uncanny way of drawing out people's stories. Often, it came as a result of simply asking questions in a caring way; at other times, it came because he offered a personal story of his own to break the ice.

"I have a civil engineering degree and hoped to find work again in Jackson. My LinkedIn profile has had many hits, but I'm not landing too many interviews. I came down here yesterday for an in-person interview and walked the streets last night to save two hundred bucks on a hotel here. It was blasted hot everywhere, even in the middle of the night. I came to the station and got a couple of hours of sleep on that bench over there. I'm sure looking forward to my own bed with my lady tonight, you know what I mean?"

Charlie looked him in the eye and gave a knowing wink. "Yup, I know all too well, young man. I was your age once and understand." The two smiled at one another and now had a connection that spanned across three generations; Jackson was young enough to be Charlie's grandson.

"Did you get lunch?" Charlie asked.

"No sir," Jackson said honestly. "I had breakfast down at Café Du Monde with a cup of coffee and a beignet."

"Can I do you the service of buying you lunch?" Charlie offered. "Or you can have the other half of my sandwich."

"Thank you, but no. My wife has let me know that she's cooking my favorite dinner as a hopeful celebration of an upcoming job. I wouldn't want to go home with no appetite, right?"

"No, I guess not," Charlie agreed. "She must be very special. What's her name?"

"Sparkle, and she does," Jackson said with a grin, then said proudly, "My son is named Jack, after me."

"Your wife's given name is really Sparkle?" Charlie asked.

"Yes, I'm not sure where her parents came up with it, but they struggled to have a baby. Sparkle came along, and since they didn't want to call her Miracle, Sparkle worked." He chuckled.

Jackson was now the curious one. “Why are you traveling by train?”

“Well, the short story is that I’m a business consultant and was here in New Orleans for a sales and marketing conference. I recently published a book about how sales were different yet the same 100+ years ago. So, I was here teaching sessions, promoting the book, and signing copies. I planned to fly to Chicago for another book reading and signing event downtown. My flight was canceled, and my cab driver suggested that I take the train instead. Since I don’t need to be in Chicago right away, and it has been a while since taking a long-distance train, I didn’t need much convincing. So here I am.”

“Man, how long is the trip to Chicago?” Jackson queried.

“I’m due into downtown Chicago tomorrow morning around 10:15 am, so if everything goes as planned, about twenty hours or so.”

Jackson felt lucky to have the short part of that ride. “It’s only four hours up to Jackson, so I’ll be going with you that far. I hope this delay isn’t too long, but I let my wife know that I might be a little longer than I’d thought.”

Charlie suddenly realized that he hadn’t told anyone of his change in plans, “Nobody is expecting me tonight in Chicago; my wife is home in Cincinnati.” He’d booked a room at the Hyatt Regency O’Hare and would need to cancel it. “I guess I better cancel the hotel reservations that I had made.” Charlie was adept at and expected travel delays. A fueling delay was just part of the program.

"That's the way it goes, I guess." Jackson was disappointed about the delay, but hopeful that he'd still be home in time for dinner, even if it was late.

Forty-five minutes passed as the two continued their conversation in the station. They exchanged histories, and Charlie shared his extensive business background with Jackson. Jackson was anxious to soak up all the details in a short amount of time, thinking they'd never see one another again. He asked about Charlie's new book, where the lessons came from, and who he'd hoped to reach in his audience. It was apparent that Jackson's degree and conversation skills would suit him well in finding a job soon.

Charlie shared an idea with Jackson that he'd been noodling on. "Wouldn't it be great if leaders could have a port in their head where they could download everything they knew about a specific subject onto a USB drive? Then the receiver could simply plug in the memory drive to themselves, upload the information, and have access to all of that experience?" Charlie came up with a term on the fly. "I'd call it human-i-pedia. Surely there would be challenges to that theory, but the way technology is going, who knows what could happen. Am I right?"

Jackson had a dazed look on his face as if he wasn't following Charlie's innovative idea.

Let's go a different direction, Charlie thought. He opened his phone and sent a LinkedIn connection request to Jackson. "I know some other people in New Orleans that may be able to help you network to a position. Would you be open to that?"

"Oh yes, that would be great Charlie! Thank you so much. I can't believe you'd be willing to do that for a total stranger."

"You're no longer a stranger, Jackson," Charlie said as he made a quick online introduction to a business friend in New Orleans on Jackson's behalf. "We're practically brothers now." Charlie and Jackson had a laugh knowing that their skin color and age difference would give it away.

An announcement came over the train station PA system:

"Train #58 to Jackson and Memphis boarding at Gate B. All passengers, please have your boarding pass and personal items with you. Sleeper car ticket holders, please line up to the left of Gate B; coach-ticketed passengers can line up to the right."

"Well, Jackson, maybe we'll see one another on board the train, but if not, keep in touch. Here is my card; look me up anytime."

"Thank you again, Charlie. Safe travels to you, and I hope everything goes well with your book signing in Chicago." Jackson headed to the train while Charlie moved quickly toward the closest restroom.

CHAPTER 2

All Aboard!

While walking down the train platform, Charlie looked up into the windows of the sleek, modern locomotive. He saw many people settling into their seats and preparing for their trip: Teenagers with earbuds like Jackson's were not paying attention to anything around them; mothers were getting their children settled; a couple of children appeared to be arguing about who got to sit next to the window.

One particular couple caught his attention because they were closer in age to him. The woman placed a small bag in the cubby above their seats while the man stared out the window as if looking for something. Charlie took a mental picture of the couple in case he saw them again. Charlie proceeded to the next train car and noticed the bright yellow safety step to board the train.

"Ticket, please," the conductor said, not letting anyone on the train without a boarding pass. Charlie obliged.

Charlie was in the second passenger car from the engine; he wanted to be close to the front to hear the train whistles.

As he climbed on board, Charlie remembered that, during college, he'd taken a job at a local amusement park to earn money for school. Because of his responsible and respectful approach during the interview, the owner gave him the job of driving the miniature train around the park. It paid a quarter more per hour, and more importantly at that time, it meant he didn't have to go around and around on the carousel or watch kids go in circles on flying saucers or little cars while he pushed the on-off buttons. It also meant that he'd get to see the other parts of the park, yell "All Aboard!" and most importantly, interact with the teenage girls that came to hang out at the amusement park.

The sound of that whistle and those teenage girls were inside his head as he placed his rolling suitcase in the storage compartment at the base of the stairway.

Charlie hoped that he'd be able to find a seat alone so that he could stretch out and be comfortable. He had traveled on hundreds of flights where he could hardly move. Charlie carried his briefcase upstairs to the coach seating. He found a suitable spot, sat next to the window, and watched the final passengers passing by. He realized that he had become one of the people others were looking at, as he remembered the older couple sitting behind him in the next car.

As he did in most situations throughout his life, Charlie quickly assessed his surroundings. There weren't any babies in his train car, which was great. He disliked flying on planes with crying children; however, young kids were a different story. He loved seeing the looks of wonder on children's faces as they flew for the first time. Charlie often traveled with Twizzlers, and this trip was no different. Many times, those 'red straws' made a parent happy when Charlie offered them to their kids on an airplane. Most of the time, the parents also took a couple for themselves.

In the seat directly in front of Charlie was a young man with his earbuds in, body leaned against the window, and already asleep. Behind him was a chatty woman with a sharp tone about her, barking instructions to someone as if they didn't know how to do what she was telling them to do. Glancing back, Charlie gave her a smile, letting her know that he was there. She continued to chatter, and he hoped the noise would stop soon and not go on for the whole 20-hour trip. Charlie laughed to himself. *No way,* he thought.

A few passengers passed Charlie in the aisle and sat in another seat. *I'll pull out a magazine and set it on the other seat to ensure nobody will sit down*, he thought to himself.

Just then, he heard, "All abooooard!" Soon, the train started slowly pulling out of the station. Charlie grabbed his phone and noted 3:45 pm. *We are running an hour late*, he thought. *Oh, I'd better text Rita and let her know that I've decided to take a train rather than fly.*

Charlie had taken this business trip without his wife this particular time. They were usually inseparable, as Rita enjoyed accompanying him. Rita also loved gardening and still worked part-time at the White Oak Gardens nursery in Cincinnati. She did so because she was knowledgeable about plants and enjoyed helping people who didn't know what they were looking for. Rita could make an uninformed customer feel comfortable and have them walking out of the store knowing more about plants than they'd ever care to know. However, it was getting to the end of the summer selling season, and Rita felt that being gone for the final weekend before the holiday wouldn't be right for the owners who had counted on her for the last ten years.

Charlie texted:

Hey Babe. Change in plans. Taking the train to Chicago rather than flying. All other plans are the same. Call when you want. I'll be traveling for 20 hours, due tomorrow morning around noon.

Charlie calculated the hour delay and figured something else would delay them a bit between here and there. “Ticket, please.” Charlie looked up, and the elderly conductor looked down at him from his great height of at least 6’ 6” tall!

"I showed you my ticket when I boarded just a couple of minutes ago." Charlie was direct and thought the process was redundant.

“Yes, sir, but we don’t know who has switched cars or gotten past one of us, and besides, I’m going to give you a paper ticket over your seat as well. It will tell us where you are getting off should you fall asleep as your stop approaches. Let’s see now, where are you headed? Says here that the name’s Charles, and you are going to Chicago.” The conductor gave him a boyish smile and a wink.

“Yes, Chicago,” Charlie said, the wink catching him off guard. “My flight was cancelled, and a local cabby suggested that I take the train instead.”

“Hmmm, that cabby’s name wouldn’t have been Aura by chance, would it?” The conductor chuckled as he inquired.

“How on earth would you know that I would have an unexpected connection with Aura?” Charlie asked in amazement.

“Just a hunch,” the conductor smiled. “My name is Mack, and if you need anything while you're on my train, Charles, you can just ask me.” Mack placed the CHI ticket above Charlie’s seat. “This ticket shows that you’re going to Chicago. If you change seats to another part of the train, be sure to have it with you. I’ll be servicing these front three cars, yup, all the way to Chicago. We have a dining car which will be open later, and a Parlour car where our guests can interact with one another or play a game while onboard. Behind that are the sleeping cars and our beautiful Sightseer car, where you can also sit leisurely with a panoramic view. Do you have any questions?” With

Charlie's shake of the head, Mack moved on to the woman on the phone.

"Excuse me, Essie, you'll have to talk in a tone that won't be disruptive to other passengers. You know that we have rules about cell phone use and bothering our neighbors around us." Charlie noticed that Mack walked past her, didn't ask for her ticket nor tell her about the train. *Odd,* he thought.

Charlie smiled, knowing he'd likely talk with Mack often during his trip to pass the time. *How did he know Aura? How did he know her name was Essie?* Charlie wasn't about to give it much thought.

Charlie had taken a cell phone snapshot of the train schedule from the website and looked at the first stop: Hammond, Louisiana, 3:45 pm. Hammond, he knew, was also an Indiana suburb of Chicago. They'd be an hour late into Hammond. It made Charlie think of the steel mills and his grandfather, who worked in East Chicago after college. But this was Hammond, Louisiana; he knew nothing about it.

The next city on the list, McComb, Mississippi, 4:32 pm, caught his attention, too. McComb, Illinois, he recalled, was home of the Western Illinois University Leathernecks, *purple,* he reminded himself. He had friends who'd gone to school there and past clients who ran their businesses there. *I haven't been to McComb in years,* he thought to himself, *but why would I?* It was one of those out-of-the-way places, and unless you had a specific purpose in going, it was off the beaten path. However, McComb, LA, was right on this train line.

Looking further down at the list of stops, Charlie was reminded of his new friend. Jackson, Mississippi,

6:44 pm. An hour's delay would put Jackson home to his wife around 8:00 pm. Late dinner, but worth it! He imagined what Jackson's wife might look like. A thin, beautiful young mom. He pictured young Jack, a family portrait, and made a mental note: *If I see him on the train, I'll have to ask to see some pictures. Should I go look for him? Rekindle the conversation from earlier? That would seem intrusive. Maybe we'll just run into each other.* Charlie left his wandering thoughts and returned to his phone to see that his power level was only 22%. He found his USB charger, plugged it into the train wall outlet, and watched the charger icon light up green.

Charlie scanned the list of stops again and realized that there were 18 between New Orleans and Chicago. Memphis, 11:40 pm, caught his attention. *We won't be there until after midnight*, he guessed. Effingham, 5:57 am. Effingham was Rita's hometown and where they'd met for the first time. Charlie's mind raced back to their first date, their time spent in Effingham, and how the two of them had moved to Cincinnati.

With the city of New Orleans behind him, the rush of the Louisiana landscape and the beautiful blue waters of Lake Pontchartrain was a distraction as Charlie thought about the wonderful times that he and Rita had experienced in their fifteen years together. Vacations and Christmas trips crossed his mind. The thought of grandkids on his shoulders made him smile. Their home in Cincinnati had become just that: *Home*. The move from Illinois found him, and Rita blessed with new friends, a late-in-life career shift into a chamber of commerce leadership role, and more time to enjoy their semi-retirement years together.

The announcement came loud and clear over the intercom:

"HAMMOND! HAMMOND, LOUISIANA IS NEXT!
NEXT STOP, HAMMOND, LOUISIANA!"

"Charlie realized that the first hour of the trip seemed to have passed in just one minute. The train appeared to slow down, and as it approached the train platform in Hammond, only a few passengers waited anxiously to board. Charlie got up and walked quickly to the doorway to get some fresh air at the first stop.

As the train came to a rest, Charlie stepped off the train into the humid afternoon heat of southern Louisiana. The onboarding passengers brushed up against him as the conductor behind him looked closely at their tickets. "We have no time for getting off the train, we will be pulling out right away. This is not a smoke stop," Mack shouted to Charlie over the loud sound of the engine.

Charlie looked out at the town in the background behind the old station. The streets were made of mud and brick. Nonetheless, the buildings weren't modern, but new. He focused on the downtown section of Hammond to see horses, wagons, and some old vehicles that looked like Model T's. Charlie blinked a couple of times, rubbed his eyes, and looked again. The town was different from how it should appear. His urge was to stay behind and check it out, but his body wouldn't move forward from the train station platform.

"All Abooooard!" Mack yelled. "Time to go!"

Charlie looked up at Mack and got back on the train. He hustled to his seat, but Hammond was gone by the time he returned to the window to check it out.

CHAPTER 3

What just happened?

Charlie felt slightly off as he started thinking about his experience at the Hammond stop. *Did I really see what I think I saw? Could the town really not have changed over the years? Was I imagining what it might have looked like in the past?* Indeed, something wasn't right. Maybe Mack would know what it was. *I'll ask him when I see him again,* Charlie thought. He checked the watch and the time felt like it was moving quickly.

Mack made his rounds through the railcar and stopped at Charlie's seat when their eyes caught one another.

"Hey Mack, when I got off the train a few minutes ago in Hammond, I had a powerful sense that I should have stayed there. My body wanted to, but my mind and your 'All aboard!' command stopped me from doing so. The town looked like it stood still in time, and I felt like I needed to check it out further. Does that make sense to you?"

Mack sat down in the empty seat next to Charlie and spoke with the authority of someone who'd seen many things in his day. "We're all busy these days, Charles. We're in a rush for the latest technology, rushing to get to the next event. We're in a hurry; the planet is in a hurry. Sometimes you just gotta sit back and take a load off and think about life. When I have a challenge in my life, I call it a 'sit on a box moment.' Then things seem clearer to me, you know?"

Charlie thought for a moment before replying to the wise conductor. "Yes, I know what you mean. I used to be a traveling salesperson, and when I was on an open road or interstate, the time with corn on my left and soybeans on my right gave me a good many answers." Charlie was in business consultant mode at this point but decided to take his curious-listener posture again. "Why do you think that is Mack?"

"That's a great question, Charles. Our country seems to be moving faster than when we were kids, you know what I mean? With an airplane, you can be anywhere on the globe in no time. The NFL is playing some games in Europe, right? Remember when there were no expressways and no interstate highways? People traveled cross-country on Route 66, Highway 1 in California, and other back roads, passing through small towns along the way. Nowadays, people choose to fly everywhere and rent a car, a convenience that not everyone can afford, but they do it anyway. Do you remember taking the train as a kid, Charles?"

"Come to think of it, I did go to Iowa with my grandmother once. We took the train from Chicago to Ft. Madison, Iowa, where I had relatives." Needing to stretch his legs, Mack got up from the seat with a calmness that showed his comfort in spending long days on this train. "My great-aunt had a farm not far from Ft. Madison, and my great-grandmother lived in a place called Farmington, in southeast Iowa, on the Des Moines River. Heard of it?"

"Yes, I know it all too well, Charles. We will talk again, but remember that when life is most challenging, people today try to hurry through their decision-making process, get to the results as fast as they can, and sometimes even flip a coin. The 23rd Psalm says: 'Yea though I walk through the valley of the shadow of death.' I've reminded people that it says 'walk,' suggesting they can take in all that is around them, learn from it, and put it to use throughout their life."

Mack stepped toward the back of the train car without pausing to say goodbye to Charlie. *I guess he just disappeared to tend to other passengers*, Charlie thought to himself. *But what of this thought of hurry in our lives? Was Aura's suggestion to take the train not as random as I may have thought? And how is Mack connected to Aura?* Charlie wondered if any of this had to do with his latest book about business lessons in 1914.

Just then, a text notification came in from Rita.

Closing today, on a break. Will call you later. The dogs are outside, and all is good here. Enjoy your train ride. Love you.

Charlie thought about the text. *Enjoy my train ride? I guess she knows that I'll make the best of every situation.* The dogs loved to be outdoors in the summer, and the fenced-in backyard allowed that to happen easily while Rita worked. He quickly replied:

Love you more!

Over the intercom came:

McCOMB! McCOMB, MISSISSIPPI IS NEXT!
NEXT STOP, McCOMB, MISSISSIPPI!

McComb was a bit larger than Hammond, and surely more people would be getting on board from there. Charlie hatched a plan. *I'll get off the train like I did in Hammond and see what McComb looks like. If it has an 'old-time' look and feel to it, I'll ask the passengers getting on about it.*

The train slowed down as it approached the next station, and Charlie got up from his seat. The woman behind him interrupted and said, "Hey, mister. What gets you on this train? You don't look like the type that would ride the train."

"What type would that be?" Charlie asked. He wasn't really curious about her answer but thought it more rhetorical and was simply being polite.

The woman continued as the train came to a stop in Hammond. "I ride this train to and from Brookhaven every day."

"You don't say! Where's Brookhaven?" Charlie was now invested in the conversation.

"Brookhaven is the next town on the line. I work for the company that cleans the N'awlins Union Station. I ride this train every day, 2 ½ hours there and back to go to work. I been doin' it for years," Her Southern accent was coming out as she got more comfortable talking with Charlie. "I ain't got nothing better to do every day, and besides, the railroad been letting me ride free for over twenty years."

"Is that right? Free?" Now Charlie was curious.

"Yeah, thass another story. I didn't have no money to travel back and forth; I'd been takin care of my mama back in Brookhaven. She's gone now. But they said since I was doing the job so well at Union Station, they'd let me ride no-charge, they called it 'gratis', until I couldn't work no longer. Mister, I ain't *never* retirin'!"

"Wait a minute, you're never going to retire because you have a free train ride to New Orleans every day?" Charlie felt confused, which was not like him. "I still don't understand."

"Sir, I seen my mama work herself to death, my daddy, too. They worked long hours. My mama was an office manager with many responsibilities. My daddy was a retail manager at the local department store. He kept it open night and day for the owner. Eventually, it done went out of business, just about the time my daddy passed. "

The woman continued, "Mama liked working for that company, but we never went on vacations or nuthin'. Me, I was what they called 'special' and couldn't get no job that paid worth a darn. I saved up my money to go to N'awlins on the train, ya see. Mama let me go alone that one time. When I got there, mmm mmmm, was I in for it. So much ta do, so much ta see! I wandered the streets and heard all sorts of jazz music. I drank liquor for the first time, too. Ain't touched it since. Well, I ran out o' money on accountta goin' down to the casino. Them slot machines were a might inviting. First, it was a nickel, then a quarta; before I knew it, I was plum out of money."

Charlie appreciated storytelling, and he was undoubtedly enthralled by hers. "What did you do? How did you get back to Brookhaven?"

"You see, God looks out for those in need. I am certain that some people were praying for me cuz I went back to Union Station without a penny in my pocket. That's when I saw a sign from God. Well, not really God, but a sign, nonetheless. It was a help-wanted sign for a custodian at Union Station. That's right, I applied right then and there. I said I was a hard worker, that I'd do whatever they asked and be grateful for the opportunity."

"You obviously got the job, didn't you?"

"Yessir! We agreed on a wage, and I began the next day."

"You started the next day?" Charlie was stunned that something like this could come about so quickly. He had not heard a story like hers in his many years of business experience. Anxious to hear more, he encouraged, "Go on."

"Well, I dint have train fare home and Mr. Martin agreed to pay it so I could tell my folks proper about the job. He said he'd pay my way back and forth as long as I continued to be a hard worker and do my best. He was a good man, that Mr. Martin. But what happened a few years later caught Mr. Martin and me by surprise. The Union Station decided to outsource — well, that's what they called it — and before you knew it, Mr. Martin was out of a job, and so was I. But then they asked me to stay after finding out how little I made. Even then, I had to take a pay cut to keep my job. But I liked what I was doin' and the people I was servin'. Passengers in N'awlins was real nice. I couldn't leave."

Charlie saw a look of hardship on the woman's face as she told the story. "So, you continued to ride the train back and forth all that time?"

"Yep, tha's right. The Amtrak folks treat me really well. I pick up a shift here or there cleaning this here train, too. I traveled by train all over the country since Mama passed. I seen the likes of the Grand Canyon and Mt. Rushmore, and I've been to see both oceans going cross country."

"I overheard you talking on your cell phone when I got on the train. Can I ask what that was all about?" Charlie started connecting the dots.

"Well, sir, I'm now in charge at Union Station. Have been for a few years now. Not everything goes smoothly, and when there's a problem, Ol' Essie's gotta tell 'em what to do. Sorry if I was disruptive - din't mean to be."

The train began moving again, and Charlie realized his opportunity to get off at McComb was missed. *Damn*, he thought to himself, *I've missed my chance to see if time had stopped there, too*. Grateful for the conversation and story with Essie, he asked a question that caught her off guard.

"Essie, in all your years, do you think that one thing stood out for you? Something that you hold on to when things get challenging?"

Essie didn't miss a beat, "Yessir. I love my God with all my might and don't work no Sundays. Tha's the Lord's Day," she continued. "And like Mr. Martin, I treat people the way I'd wanna be treated. He told me that's the Golden Rule."

With that, Charlie appeared to be blown away by her story. *Don't judge a book by its cover or your first impressions,* he thought. *A-ha! That's why Mack knew her name. She's been riding this train for years, and I remember now that he seemed to know her when he asked her to be quiet on the phone.* It was all coming together.

As the train rumbled down the tracks, the loudspeaker announced:

"BROOKHAVEN! BROOKHAVEN,
MISSISSIPPI IS NEXT!
NEXT STOP, BROOKHAVEN, MISSISSIPPI!"

Chapter 4

Dining Car

Charlie said a pleasant goodbye to Essie as she got up to leave the train. Cordial as it was, he figured that their paths would never cross again. Charlie should have given her a business card or gotten her information. However, it did cross his mind that if he ever got to the New Orleans Union Station again, he'd have to look her up.

After Brookhaven came Hazlehurst, Mississippi, and with Charlie's A.D.D. came fresh ideas and new thoughts. He'd already forgotten about his eerie encounter in Hammond, and his stomach started talking to him again. That turkey sandwich was hours ago.

Charlie pulled out his large family-size bag of Twizzlers and began going seat to seat from the front of the car to the back, offering to his left and right like a flight attendant might on a plane. Several young kids and parents appreciated the gesture; some put up a hand as if to say, 'No, thank you.' Charlie received more than one strange face, recognizing that what he did wasn't typical for a train ride like this. With the train rolling down the track at high speed, he gripped each corner of the seat backs to steady himself. Charlie wasn't a Spring chicken any longer but was still agile for a 70-year-old. When he got to the back of the car, he still had some Twizzlers remaining, but had he started into the next car, he might not have had any left for the remainder of the trip.

The seat beside him was still empty, and Charlie felt lucky to have the extra space to himself so far. As he looked at the time on his phone, they were still behind the train timetable schedule. At this pace, they would arrive in Jackson, Mississippi, at about 7:30 pm.

"APPROACHING HAZLEHURST, MISSISSIPPI!"

The train slowed down as it had with the previous stops, but this approach to the Hazlehurst station seemed different for some reason. The train slowed to a snail's pace, and the whistle blew louder than Charlie had noticed previously. WOOOOOO – WOOOOOO! WOOO – WOOOOOO! Two longs, a short and followed by another long whistle. That's the universal sign for coming through a crossing, Charlie recalled from working at the amusement park. As the train engineer sounded the horn, the train quickly sped up to 80 miles per hour.

Just then, Mack appeared to announce that the dining car was now open and that it was five cars behind Charlie's.

"Mack, what happened with that last stop? We didn't stop, did we?"

Mack was ready with his answer, "No, Charles, we had no scheduled passengers getting on or off; it is known as a flag stop. We slowed down for safety reasons, and with the history and circumstances there in Hazlehurst, we look for people waiting for the next train, ready to stop if we need to do so."

Charlie again took in what Mack said but grew curious. "What happened there? What circumstances?"

"May I sit down a minute, Charles? I don't want to startle the other passengers. You see, about fifteen years ago, during the financial crisis in our country…"

"The great recession," Charlie chimed in.

"Exactly. Well, a young fella who had a wife and a couple of young children felt that there was no alternative but to assure his family would be taken care of with a life insurance policy."

"You mean he…" Charlie followed.

"Yes, he fell on the tracks just as the train was coming into town. The train was late that particular day, and, in the winter, darkness falls far sooner than it does right now. Mr. Potts, our engineer, didn't see him at all but knew that something wasn't right."

"Oh, man! I had an uncle who committed suicide, or so it is believed. Terrible circumstances for those who are left behind. How did your engineer deal with the situation?"

Mack felt compelled to change the course of the conversation, "Mr. Potts was fine, eventually. He got counseling and was close to retirement anyway. He retired with a full pension, and I haven't talked to him for several years. What happened next in the town was shocking. I understand everyone in town picked up the cause for the man's wife and family. Money was raised, and they were not just taken care of by the funds from the life insurance company but emotionally by the community. Thankfully, the wife was able to find love again, and I understand that they have survived as a family."

"I'd always heard that suicide was a long-term solution to what is often a short-term problem." Charlie continued. "However, I know that the word 'solution' is a bad one to use. Sorry about that."

"Yes, Charles, God is the one who is intended to bring life and death to the world, but free will is something that all people have, and it is a gift from God. No, not intended for taking one's life in this way." A tear came to Mack's face as he continued to the front of the train to tell others that the dining car was now open.

Charlie was very emotional when he got up from his seat. Heading to the dining car, his knees were wobblier than ever before. The rolling back and forth of the train cars, especially when he moved from car to car, was particularly challenging. As he came to the train car connections, the heat of the day was met with the whisp of wind carrying the train northward. As he entered the next car, the cool air conditioning hit him with that same feeling as when one enters their home on a sweltering summer afternoon. Five times Charlie hit the heat between each train car and the coolness of the next train car before getting to his destination, the dining car.

Upon arrival, the seating area was about half-filled. Charlie was greeted by the dining steward. “How many, sir?”

“I am dining alone unless you have a fair maiden in your car who needs a companion?” Charlie chuckled at his bold and playful approach with someone he’d never met.

“We seat individual guests with another to be efficient, sir. If you’d like, there’s a woman directly over there who is seated alone. Would you like to join her?”

Charlie gulped and hadn't really thought of such a proposition being available, especially asking in such a playful way. Her back was turned to him, so there was no way to tell what she looked like. She had long dark hair flowing down past her shoulders and appeared to be sitting with good posture; why he noticed that, Charlie didn’t know.

“Sure, I’d be glad to join her,” Charlie said.

The anticipation of meeting a mysterious woman on a train intrigued Charlie, but only for the ten seconds it took to cross the dining car. “Your name, sir?” she asked.

"My name is Charlie, ma’am; may I join you for dinner?” Charlie was always the gentleman.

“You may. I’m Jessica. Pleased to meet you, Charlie.” Jessica appeared to be in her 40’s, was professionally dressed in a dark blue business suit with a pure white ruffled blouse. She didn’t get up to greet Charlie but offered her hand with a firm handshake. “Where is your final destination, Charlie?”

"I'm going to Kansas City...Kansas City, here I come." Charlie responded in tune; he had a great singing voice. “I’m going to Jackson, gonna mess around.” Charlie turned on his charm with his best Johnny Cash rendition. “Thank you...thank you very much. I’m Johnny Cash.” He smiled playfully.

“With an approach like that, you’ll surely land yourself in Folsom Prison!” Jessica smiled back. Charlie felt like he was blushing just a little.

“Well, I’ll be available if you need anything,” said the steward as he exited quietly.

As the time passed and dinner was served, Charlie would learn that Jessica was a successful and seasoned saleswoman trying to make it in a man's world. She sold industrial tools and was heading to Jackson, Mississippi, for a meeting the next day. Unmarried and living in Chicago, she rode this train route occasionally because she had a monthly rail pass that allowed for stops along the way at a much lower cost.

Charlie thought he would be charming. “I can’t believe that I’d be sitting here with another Chicagoan... On a train bound for nowhere... I heard you met up with a gambler... And you were both too tired to sleep”. Charlie breaking into song in the middle of dinner was even too corny for Jessica, who groaned at the childish approach. She did give him kudos for his impersonation of Kenny Rogers, but that was it.

"Jessica, tell me something," he continued. "I've been in business environments for fifty years and have seen a great many changes in that time, especially for professional women like yourself. What has kept you going, and what advice would you give someone like my granddaughter who'd like to be a businesswoman someday?" Charlie had obviously put his playful nature away in favor of his inquisitive self. "I have been in leadership and sales most of my life. Jessica, what has helped you most in your sales career?"

"Honestly, Charlie, if that's your real name." She winked playfully. "People are where they are. Some people need help making buying decisions; others know what they're looking for already. The internet has helped a great deal, and 70% of people have already checked out our website before they even reach out these days. That makes my job easier than you probably had it when you were getting started, am I right?"

"You are, Jessica. It was all about cold calling and closing techniques back in the day. Zig Ziglar was one of the best, and I've read many of his books several times." Charlie had an extensive business book library in his office. He was in his element now.

"People don't care how much you know..." Jessica started.

Charlie finished the saying, "...Until they know how much you care." Both had to laugh at the charming moment.

"My dad was a salesman who bought all of Zig's tapes. They're now all available online and on YouTube." Jessica continued. "He instilled in me the desire to win, but not to win at all costs. He was focused on one person at a time and came up in an era before CRM systems existed. I don't know how successful he would have been had he been able to access HubSpot or Salesforce; maybe he wouldn't have embraced the technology. We'll never know. He was a good man, though, and taught me a great deal about life."

"Sounds like a great guy. I would have enjoyed meeting him. Can I assume he passed away?" Charlie asked very delicately.

"Yes. He smoked too much, drank too much, and played very hard. Worked hard, played hard." Jessica knew by Charlie's facial expression he knew what she was talking about. She continued, "Charlie, you are so easy to talk with; thank you for listening. I generally don't open up like this to someone that I just met." A chance meeting in a dining car was just what she needed at that point.

They exchanged stories as the dinner service continued. Jessica shared that she'd been married once but was now divorced, had two grown children, and just hadn't found the right guy. Well, a second one, anyway. Charlie pulled out his phone to share pictures of Rita, their children, and the grandkids. Jessica looked at the pictures with great interest. "Do you love them all the same? How can you do that with so many of them?"

"Your love expands to fill them, not the other way around. When a new one comes into our lives, we carve out another piece of our heart for them."

Jessica needed to hear these particular words and began sharing from her heart. "My dad was loving and caring, but my mom never accepted me for who I was. After my dad died, she became reclusive, self-centered, and didn't care enough to be in my kid's lives. That hurts me, and I know that it has hurt my kids." Jessica was on the verge of tears.

Charlie explained, "You must be patient with parents, kids, and with virtually all relationships, for that matter. Someday, she may realize what you've known for some time. She may not, but you have to know in your heart that you have done what is right for you and your relationships. When times are most challenging, I have to say that patience usually plays in my favor. Continue to tell your kids and parents that you love them. That seems easy, but it often is not."

Jessica understood what Charlie was saying, "But it's so hard when she's... you know... a pain in the...". Jessica was conscious of her openness. "I don't mean to be angry... she just can be."

"I get it and understand more than you'd know. Hopefully, the relationship will come around with some time and your hard work. For you first and then your kids... maybe?" Charlie shrugged his shoulders, taking a posture of helpfulness but obviously not knowing all the details of Jessica's life to understand fully.

"Hey, Charlie!" a familiar voice shouted over the sound of the train and background music.

"Jackson!" Charlie shouted back. "Are we there yet?"

Jessica didn't understand the remark, but clearly Jackson did. "My lady is getting the kids to bed, has dinner waiting, and we are going to celebrate!"

"Celebrate what?" Jessica was now interested in the details.

"My young friend Jackson interviewed for an engineering job in New Orleans. We met at Union Station, and he's heading home to Jackson, Mississippi. I think it's the next stop."

"Charlie...no, we're going to celebrate that I GOT the job in New Orleans! I received an email since we talked earlier, and they would like me to start in two weeks." Jackson was clearly over-the-moon excited.

"What firm will you be with?" Jessica asked.

"Marlow, Egleston, Anderson, and Nelson is the name of the engineering firm. Why do you ask?"

"As it turns out, my connections in New Orleans are wide and varied, and I know several people at that firm. In fact, I know many people in the Big Easy that I can introduce when the time is right. How 'bout that?"

"Yes, ma'am, that would be incredibly kind of you. Do you have a business card that I could have?" Jackson was polite but direct in asking Jessica for her card. She reached into her leather purse and pulled one out for him without hesitation.

Charlie's mind was still thinking about the firm's name as if it were a word puzzle. "Oh, I get it now," he interrupted the otherwise professional conversation between Jackson and Jessica. "The firm's initials make up the word M-E-A-N. Jackson, I can't see you working for a MEAN company, but you'll have to do what you have to," The three laughed.

"JACKSON! JACKSON, MISSISSIPPI, NEXT!
NEXT STOP, JACKSON, MISSISSIPPI!"

It became clear that the three new friends needed to go their separate ways. Jessica picked up Charlie's dinner bill and asked him to pay it forward sometime on her behalf. The three of them said their final goodbyes and ended in song as Charlie coaxed them to do....

"I'm the train they call The City of New Orleans...I'll be gone five hundred miles when the day is done..."

The dining car cheered as the three strutted away like rock stars.

Chapter 5

Jackson

Charlie made his way back through the five passenger cars; however, this time, he felt light on his feet, gliding between the cars, not noticing the heat he'd felt earlier and almost dancing through the aisles of each moving train car. He felt the emotional bond with Jackson and Jessica carry him and the rush of newfound friends exhilarating. Charlie sat down in his coach car seat and took a breath.

As happens when one least expects it, magic appears. Sometimes, that magic is in the form of a key employee joining an organization at the right time; other times, an offer for your house exceeds the listing price. Charlie recalled such a moment when a ticket to see the Cleveland Indians became available through one of his previous business partners. It was not just to see the Indians, but rather who they were playing that came with it. The year was 2016, and the bonus came as a ticket to Game 7 of the World Series to see his beloved Chicago Cubs.

Charlie thought back to that night and that phone call. He'd taken and made thousands of calls over his career. "Yes, that's my answer. Yes, I'm in. Without a doubt, count me in. Thank you so much. I will see you tomorrow in Cleveland. Again, I can't thank you enough." That's all he could recall; detailed instructions had long since been forgotten. Dropping what was on his plate that day could have been challenging; however, for a chance to see Chicago baseball history happen in person, the answer was easy.

He recalled how he felt that week and how the entire city was buzzing about the Cubs in 2016. The exhilaration of the Cubs World Series was among his lifetime highlights, but as with the Cubs, there were plenty of low times as well.

As Charlie looked out the window at an evening sky that was brilliant with its red, orange, and purple glow on this late June evening, his mind raced to many of the business challenges he'd encountered over his long life. Financial struggles during times of unemployment were challenging to navigate as the sole provider for the family. Charlie recalled hiring the wrong person for a key position on more than one occasion; those decisions were setbacks that were hard to overcome. He could almost feel the knots in his stomach return as he thought about the lawsuit he was involved with early in his career.

However, Charlie was the eternal optimist; everything seemed to work out as it was supposed to, and if he was honest about it, there was always a life lesson that came from those challenging times. His wife Rita had told him that things always work out for the best. If she said it once, she would say it a million times. Well, not a million, maybe a hundred.

The thought of Rita warmed his heart; he was still madly in love with this woman. Still in the honeymoon phase after 15 short years, he thought. Gazing out the window again, Charlie noticed the country landscape had turned urban; Jackson, Mississippi, appeared in the distance with the evening sky aglow.

Charlie could see Mack rushing through the car toward him, "Mack, why are you in such a rush?" Charlie noted that the otherwise steady conductor had a bounce in his step. "What's the matter?" he asked.

"I just got word that we will have an unscheduled delay in Jackson because of a freight train breakdown and occupying the track to the north. I need to find out what the next steps are. Can't talk right now, Charles. Wait for a train announcement or ask me when I return in this direction." Mack turned and continued toward the front of the train.

Other passengers had overheard the brief conversation and started talking amongst themselves over the tops of the seats. What had been an otherwise orderly ride became more chaotic. Stories of past experiences began to flow.

"These freight companies, they have no consideration for those of us on passenger trains! I was traveling from New Orleans to Houston once, and it seemed like it took days to get there with all the freight train delays." The woman across the aisle shared loudly enough for several people around her to hear. "If this turns into another fiasco like that, I'm never riding a train again." She was animated beyond measure.

Charlie had seen stressful situations like this over his lifetime of business travel. Running through airports, missed flights, car breakdowns, and hotel debacles of all sorts came to mind. While each was different, often after the fact, they were laughable, but rarely in the moment. *We'll just have to wait and see what comes of this one*, he thought.

The train had come to a complete stop as an announcement came over the loudspeaker:

"Attention! Attention all passengers! We have arrived in Jackson, Mississippi. All passengers with Jackson as their final destination may disembark at this time. Our crew will assist you and answer any questions. We anticipate an 11:30 pm departure. If you are a ticketed passenger continuing to travel north, you may leave the train with proper identification and your ticket, allowing you to reboard this train and this train only. You must be onboard no later than 11:15 pm Central Time in order to continue your trip. If you choose to stay on the train and move about, be sure to have your ticket with you for verification if asked by a crew member. Thank you for your patience; we apologize for the untimely delay."

Charlie immediately thought about his newfound friend Jackson, who must be ecstatic that the freight train breakdown happened in his hometown and not sooner. *He'll still get to have dinner with his wife,* Charlie thought happily. With all the hustle that would surely ensue, Charlie would not have a chance to find Jackson and wish him well, but the parting in the dining car just a few minutes earlier filled him with joy. *What about Jessica?* he thought. Should he look for her to share the time in Jackson with? He didn't even know what car she was in.

Grabbing his phone, which was now fully charged, Charlie put his ticket in his back left pocket for safekeeping. When traveling, Charlie always kept hotel keys and important papers in his back left pocket out of habit, so he'd always know where to find them.

Everyone in Charlie's car was milling about, trying to decide whether to get off or stay aboard the train. Charlie stayed seated as he often did on airplanes. *No sense being in a hurry*. While a few remained in their seats, most passengers were soon gone when he looked around his rail car. When the aisles were clear, he went to the door, where a different conductor helped him step off the train and onto the platform. *Where's Mack?* he wondered to himself. He had never returned through the train after hustling through earlier. *Hmmm, I'll have to learn about this holdup when I get back,* Charlie thought to himself.

Charlie slowly made his way down the platform of the historic train station. Not knowing whether to head north or south, he decided to go inside the station and see if they had any updated information on the delay. Charlie pushed through the beautiful stained-glass doors and noticed that there wasn't a rush of cool air. *No air conditioning,* he thought to himself. He made his way downstairs, passing beautiful long hardwood pews made by craftsmen back in the day. Charlie wondered who had passed through this old station over the years. Now, however, the station was void of people. It was empty, quiet, and dimly lit as the night sky began to descend.

Charlie walked through the station, down the steps to the set of doors on the opposite side of the building and pushed through to see where they were leading. The state capitol building was in front of him, but it had a strange aura about it. Charlie saw cobblestone streets, buildings, and architecture that reminded him of some old streets in Chicago where the architecture stood the test of time. Here, wood structures were everywhere. As his senses took over, the sound of horse hooves and carts grabbed his attention. Gas lamplights were lit, people were still in the streets, and nighttime was upon the town. The townspeople were dressed differently.

Charlie recalled his experience earlier at the Hammond stop. Something was amiss. He continued down the cobblestone road toward what he thought might be the main street. He walked through a dark alleyway and could see a light at the end. He felt compelled to continue his search for answers.

When Charlie arrived at the main street, he looked to his left. One neon sign lit the street; it simply said HARDWARE. A couple of the other shops appeared to still be open, but most were not, as it was getting late in the evening. Red, white, and blue bunting was everywhere. Looking to the right, he could see more shops and another neon sign at the top of a much larger building that read: GRAND HOTEL. Not wanting to appear too conspicuous, Charlie reached for his cell phone in his pocket to take a selfie. However, the phone was dead, with no service and a blank screen. Charlie knew that he'd charged the phone earlier. He tried to restart the phone, but that didn't help the situation. *Strange*, he thought.

Again, he recalled his experience earlier in the day and wondered if there was a connection. Charlie passed by the windows of the local department store only to find displays foreign to him— items that one wouldn't see today; rather, items from an era long passed.

As he crossed the cobblestone street, Charlie's sights were on the Grand Hotel. Around him, black thin-wheeled pickup trucks and model-T Fords lined the roads, but none were moving. Horse-drawn carriages were abundant among the handful of motor vehicles. *There are no foreign cars here!* Charlie laughed out loud as he thought about the strange situation, he found himself in. *I guess I can embrace it or deny it* he thought. *Is this a dream?* He reached into his back pocket; yes, his ticket was still there, too.

Standing at the entrance to the Grand Hotel was a Black man wearing a red blazer and hat.

"May I help you sir?" He appeared to be addressing Charlie directly. "May I help you? You ain't got no bags. You look to be a stranger to these parts."

"Where are we?" Charlie inquired in a puzzled manner. "Is this Jackson, Mississippi?"

“Oh, yes sir, Jackson alright. You think you were somewhere else?”

"No, I just..." Charlie paused and could see that the doorman was genuinely interested in helping. "Is there a hotel manager inside?"

"Yes, sir. You are looking for Mr. Aberdeen. He’s your man. You can find him at the front desk, and if he ain’t there, ask Julius to fetch him right quick.”

“Much obliged.” Charlie realized that he’d never used the word obliged before; it just seemed appropriate.

As Charlie walked up the hotel entrance stairs, he marveled at the craftsmanship all around him. The carved woodwork on the entry railing was magnificently detailed. The chandelier sparkled with a brilliance he’d only seen at such elegant places as the Waldorf Astoria in New York and the Palmer House Hotel in Chicago.

His recollection of the Palmer House made him think of barbequed ribs at Miller’s Pub. *That’s odd; I haven’t thought about Miller’s for a long time,* he noted as he continued up the stairs.

A woman who appeared in a formal, deep navy-blue dress and who was in charge behind the registration desk addressed Charlie, “May I help you, sir?”.

“I am looking for a Mr. Aberdeen. Do you know where I might find him?” Charlie asked.

The woman turned to her colleague. “Julius, where might Mr. Aberdeen be this evening?”

Obviously, Julius must be in charge of Mr. Aberdeen’s whereabouts. He was smartly dressed in a three-piece pinstriped suit and coordinated solid navy blue tie. His shirt collar was pressed, and his black shoes shined.

“He’s gone over to the hardware store but will return shortly.”

“This man is looking for Mr. Aberdeen. Can you please speak with him?” The woman removed herself from the conversation and disappeared down the hotel hallway.

Charlie stepped forward in awe. “Yes, I was told Mr. Aberdeen was the manager of this beautiful hotel. It is impeccable, by the way. Everything looks so new.”

“We just built the place a few years ago. Ain’t got the shine off it yet. I am Julius; I am at your service. Mr. Aberdeen will be back shortly, but in the meantime, how can I be of assistance, sir? Are you looking for a room tonight?”

"No, sir. I was riding the train north to Chicago from New Orleans, and the train was delayed. It was as if I stepped back in time when I got off. What year is it? We are in Jackson, right? Jackson, Mississippi?"

“Yes sir, Jackson alright. 1914, June 30th, in fact. Lived here all my life,” Julius was sure of himself on this matter but was puzzled about the stepped back in time comment. “Where did you say you came from? New Orleans? Are you staying here in Jackson?”

“Staying in Jackson? No, I don’t think so. I’m not sure how all of this has happened, 1914, wow!” Charlie shook his head with a look of wonder. “As I said, our train is simply delayed, and somehow, I’ve stepped back in time. Hopefully, we’ll be on our way soon enough. I’m heading to Chicago. You may not believe it, but it’s the truth… My name is Charlie.”

Unsure of what Julius thought, Charlie tried to gauge the look on his face, but the man was unflappable.

"You don't say, Charlie? Well then, we are about to have us a conversation. Come into the parlor where we can get comfortable. Can I get you a drink before we get started?"

Considering the year and circumstances he found himself in, Charlie answered in good form. "Some whiskey would be nice — if you have ice, even better."

"Oooo, hmmm! We got ice; yes, sir, we do. We were the first business back in our original building down the street to have an ice machine in Jackson; seems a long time ago. Ice making, among other things, made us different than other hotels. Mr. Aberdeen built the Grand because he wanted to serve more guests. He doubled the number of rooms and added every convenience we could think of," Julius explained with pride in his voice. "I will be right back."

Julius returned quickly with two glasses and handed one to Charlie. "Here's to us and... what year did you say you came from? Woo, doggy, I definitely need this drink as much as you do!" Julius had an infectious smile. "Start at the beginning; I don't want to miss any details of this adventure you're talking about."

Charlie reached into his pocket and pulled out his phone. "You see this? Where I come from it has every piece of information you could EVER imagine on it. In fact, if it were working, I could look up 'Jackson, Mississippi', and '1914' and find all the information I wanted. I could search for the train schedule on here. See how much you charge for a room per night. I could investigate what people thought of your fine hotel and even make a reservation from this device!"

"You could do what? All of those things? What do you mean?" Julius was an inquisitive listener at this point. "I gotta have a printed train schedule in my hand to know when the train will be passing through. I have a rate card that tells me how much the rooms cost; they's different right now. Higher, that is, on account of the Independence Day celebration. It's been nearly fifty years since the end of the War Between the States; I was born in 1865. My papa came home after all the fighting, and my mama, she just started having babies; I'm the first of 8 children she bore."

"You don't say." Charlie couldn't believe what he was hearing, but he was one to experience whatever life threw his way. "So, your father fought in the war, huh? What does he do now?"

"My dad passed many years ago. My mother was left to raise us kids alone. She married my father's younger brother on account of needing to support us kids. He's a good man, Mr. Aberdeen is."

"Wait a minute!" Charlie had a shocked look on his face. "Mr. Aberdeen, is your stepfather? THE Mr. Aberdeen who owns this hotel?"

"Yes, sir, it was my uncle who married my mama. I aim to be in charge here someday. Mr. Aberdeen's been training me to take over when he's too tired to run it anymore. If you're wondering, I call him Dad when we're away from the hotel." Julius wanted Charlie to know that detail. "What kind of work do you do, Charlie?"

"Julius, I am a writer and business consultant, someone who helps people like yourself and your dad with various business challenges. I do that in numerous ways, but mostly through conversation and helping them see where they can make improvements. Some call me a business therapist." Charlie realized he had gone down a path he should not have with Julius. "I mean, most businesses have challenges; that's not to say yours does. I have even written about how business was conducted back in 1914."

"No offense taken, Charlie. We could have used your help many times over the years. We are currently trying to figure out how I can earn my way into owning this place. I have two siblings left, and both expect an inheritance from Mr. Aberdeen." Julius stopped to let Charlie speak.

Charlie felt compelled to clarify before proceeding with the conversation. "Wait...did you just say TWO siblings? I thought you had seven brothers and sisters, isn't that right?"

"Yes, but there's only three of us left. Life in the South has been tough. I could tell you each of their stories, but yes, it is me, my one brother, and a sister who are left for Mr. Aberdeen —I mean—DAD, to take care of," Julius explained. "My sister married well. Mary's husband, Thomas, owns the hardware store where Mr. Aberdeen has gone. My brother? Well, there's a different story. Blake, he's a plumber. He has more work than he can handle in his own business. This indoor plumbing has created all sorts of opportunities. He just doesn't know how to manage people or his business. My brother-in-law, Thomas, has tried to help him, but Blake doesn't want to listen to him. I've given up trying."

"I hadn't anticipated having this conversation, Julius. I was looking to see where I was and what was happening. I had no idea that I'd land in 1914, potentially ready to answer your business questions. Most people need someone to coach them, a mentor who can help lead them down the path. Do you know what I mean, Julius?"

"Oh yes, Mr. Aberdeen has been working with me these last few years. He's taught me more than I could ever have known going to college. I worked at various places. Did a good many things before coming here to the Grand Hotel. I think that those opportunities played a part in helping me decide that this is what I was meant to do."

"Do you feel that way, Julius? Like you are meant to be here at the Grand Hotel?" The answer to his question was interrupted.

"I understand that you are looking for me. I'm Mr. Aberdeen." The hotel owner was confident looking, well-tailored, and seemed pleased that Julius had shown Charlie some hospitality, "Pleasure to meet you. What is your name?"

"My name is Charlie. Thank you for seeing me. Julius was sharing some background about the Grand Hotel." Charlie stood up, and the two men clasped hands, as all business professionals have done throughout the decades.

"Well, I don't know what he's told you, but I'm sure it's all true. Not a dishonest bone in this man's body," Aberdeen bragged about Julius.

Charlie followed the statement up, “Julius tells me that you are looking to transition the Grand Hotel to him as you begin to work less. Is that right?” Charlie was in consultant mode and felt compelled to be direct.

“That’s correct. You and I are of similar age, so surely you understand the importance of handing things off properly. If you aren’t planning for your future, it’s likely to run over you like an eight-horse hitch wagon. I have been showing Julius ‘the ropes’ for the last few years, and I think he’s ready to take over.”

Julius seemed surprised at the comment as if they had not discussed a final timeline to make the transition official. “Are you serious? We had not talked about when that would happen or how to make it work financially with Blake and Mary.”

"Details, son, we'll work on the details. I have all the confidence in the world in you. You have learned from other positions you’ve held, proving yourself time and time again with me and our employees. On top of that, you continue to study about new things in our business on your own time. Yes, I know about those books you read and the ideas you have in your head. Don’t think that I haven’t thought about them, too. I'm starting to feel my age these days and want to make sure that our guests are taken care of. You will do fine. Mister…?”

“You can call me Charlie,” he reminded him.

“Charlie, how old are you?” Aberdeen asked inquisitively.

“I am 70 years young,” Charlie retorted. “Why do you ask?”

"Charlie, I see you have a drink in your hand, and now is a time of celebration. Independence Day is celebrated on the 4th of July, our independence from England in the Revolution, and nearly fifty years since the end of the War Between the States. Many battles were won and lost. Many people died in both of those wars. We have a long way to go before we're healed from the wounds of that fighting. I know that I am in the minority here in Jackson, but the Black man needs to be lifted up. They have had family losses too. Many white folks here in the South don't understand that a person's skin color doesn't matter any more than their upbringing or lineage. I got kinfolk that ain't worth a darn, and they are as white as white can be. Makes them no better or worse than anyone else, not as far as I see it."

Julius was amazed that Aberdeen would choose to share that at this particular moment. "I agree with you, Dad," it came out naturally. "Charlie, we pay our people the same no matter their color or whether they are men or women. We got a woman cleaning manager who wants to have her own business someday. George, the doorman out front, makes more than most people because he's good with our guests. He makes generous tips, but because he's got a family to feed, we want him to be able to take care of his youngins."

"Son, how many times have I told you not to call me Dad here at the hotel?" Aberdeen had a twinkle in his eye when he said it.

Charlie jumped in. "You are his dad, and I can see that you two have mutual respect for one another, common values, and love between you, which is admirable in any family-owned business." Charlie continued, "Time is upon me, and while I feel compelled to stay and continue this conversation, my train awaits. Before I go, I'd like to impart to the two of you something that comes from my years of experience. But first, let me ask if your hotel has a mission statement. Do you know what a mission statement is?"

Julius was prepared to respond. "Follow me," he said, and the three got up from the parlor and walked into the Grand's lobby. "Charlie, Dad and I put this saying in a frame just last year. It reads: 'We take care of our employees so they can care for you while you stay at the Grand Hotel. We will do our best to help you rest.' It didn't take long for us to write. We sat down and intentionally built a budget last year. Yes, we have a budget, too. Finally, Dad and I discussed how important repeat guests are and how quality service helps them share our story with others. We are the most preferred hotel in Jackson," Julius boasted proudly.

Aberdeen took control of the conversation. "Charlie, I don't know how you found your way to the Grand Hotel, but just hearing my son talk about our hotel that way in front of you makes me proud beyond measure. While we can't, by law, serve black guests just yet, we hope to do so soon. As I shared, we are in good hands, and I will be able to step away knowing that Julius has it under control. Yes, I'll be here if he needs me, but otherwise, you may find me in New Orleans enjoying a drink and some jazz music more often than I would otherwise." He smiled and appeared satisfied as one feels after a good hearty meal.

Julius offered his hand as a gesture to say goodbye too. "Dad, I'll fill you in on where Charlie came from after he's left. Trust me, you will think it outrageous, but you'll have to believe me."

"Goodbye, Julius and Mr. Aberdeen. You have much to be proud of and are blessed beyond measure. In my years of working with business owners, I can say that your story is among the best I've heard; you have done well and will continue to do so. Thank you for the hospitality and the drink."

Charlie's stay at the hotel didn't give him the rest that Aberdeen and Julius spoke about; in fact, he was more excited than ever about his faith in business leadership and succession planning. He retraced his steps on the cobblestone street and asked a passerby if they had the time. Recognizing that he didn't have too much time before he needed to be back at the train station, he recalled that Julius had mentioned that his brother-in-law owned the local hardware store. Charlie wondered how different it would be from a modern Home Depot or Lowes. Thomas was the name of the owner. He said it out loud several times in order to remember — it was a technique he'd used for years. *"Tom, Thomas, Tom, Thomas. I'll ask for Thomas."*

The store would be easy enough to find. Its neon sign had a warm glow and an appeal to it among the otherwise dark stores on the main street. Charlie approached the building, wondering whether they would be open at this hour or whether Thomas was still there. *We'll have to see,* he thought to himself.

As he approached the hardware store, the sign in the window said CLOSED. People must know when they're open. Pressing his face to the door window as he tried the knob, he confirmed that it was locked; however, he saw a man inside, appearing to be counting something on the countertop. Charlie knocked on the door to get the man's attention and he waved in a friendly sort of way. *Here he comes,* Charlie saw and considered what he would say.

"Good evening, I'm sorry to trouble you, but I just came from the Grand Hotel where I'd met Mr. Aberdeen and his son Julius. You wouldn't be Thomas by chance?" Charlie was unsure if he'd be the owner or not.

"Sure am. I don't normally open the door to strangers this time of night, but you have an honest look about you. I pretty much know everyone in town. Everyone needs something from here, sometimes I got it, other times I don't. You need something?" It was apparent that if Charlie did need something, Thomas would do what he could to help him find it.

"No, I really don't need anything unless you have something to fix my phone." Charlie began pulling the cell phone from his pocket and chuckled. "I guess you wouldn't know anything about it. Sorry, bad joke on my part." Charlie thought about what year it was, and because of his book research, he knew that the telephone existed, but it was years behind the cellular era. "I can't stay long, but Aberdeen and Julius said that you might still be here. Looks like you are finishing inventory. As I said, I don't want to stay long, but I've worked with retail hardware stores back where I come from." Recognizing that it was 1914,

Charlie went out on a limb to ask, “Do you have a telephone here at the store?”

"Yes, sir! A brand new one, as a matter of fact. Never saw the need to have one but it seems everyone’s getting one installed for their businesses. I’ve had it for about a month. Why did you ask about my new telephone? Are you sure that you don’t need nuthin’?”

Charlie thought about how to continue the conversation; he was curious to see what the place looked like and how it compared with some of the independent hardware stores that he’d worked with over the years. His instincts kicked in regarding the use of a phone. "Where I come from, everyone has a telephone, but they don't have wires attached to them." Charlie stopped dead in his tracks. Was he really going to describe satellites, wave technology, video, and the internet to someone from 1914? *What a terrible idea,* he decided. "What made you get a telephone for your business?" The question was a natural progression and a conversational pivot that was comfortable for him.

“The salesman who came to see me had his pitch well prepared. I didn’t have a chance to say no. He asked me lots of questions, had impressive answers and before I knew it, my telephone connected my business with other businesses here in Jackson. Not many people have them in their homes yet, but I’ll be ready when they do. Well, that’s what the salesman said anyway.”

He laughed and continued. “I have a profitable business and have grown into this space with more inventory. That’s both good and bad. I’m busier each month, and everyone knows that I’ve probably got what they're looking for, so they pass the word on to others. The other hardware store down the road even sends customers my way if they ain't got what the customer is looking for. Now the hardware suppliers have already started to call the shop on my telephone. I have to stop what I'm doing and go to the back office, where the phone is - it's a bother. I wish that telephone was more convenient." The two walked casually through the store, and Charlie marveled at the cleanliness of such a large store.

"I can tell you that the telephone will be more convenient someday. Maybe not in your lifetime. Hopefully, it will benefit you the way the salesman said."

"Embrace the innovation, is that what you're saying?" Thomas felt comfortable enough to ask.

"I would tell you to do so whenever it logically makes sense. Sometimes you just have to go with your gut. You know what I mean by that?" Charlie asked.

"Yes, I have used my instincts plenty; that's why we have a neon sign out front. Among the first ones in town. The same as what happened with the telephone, when the sign salesman came by asking if I wanted to be on the cutting edge."

Smart move, Charlie thought as Thomas continued.

"I also ask my customers for their opinions on a regular basis and what they want to see for sale in my store. I've talked with other store owners in small towns from here to N'awlins. They've helped me, and I've helped them figure out the best ideas for our shops in different towns." Thomas was beaming with pride about his store.

“I can certainly confirm that your approach is sound. It is called a best practice.” Charlie sounded like a consultant.

"Mister, you must know what you're talking about, but I have no idea whether you're coming or going. It's getting late, and I must finish this small goods inventory. Was there something else you needed?"

Charlie gave the man another firm handshake. "My name is Charlie, and if you see Julius or Mr. Aberdeen, please tell them we talked. Thanks for showing me around your place. It’s a mighty fine hardware store you have.”

Suddenly Charlie was aware of the time passing. “What time do you have?” With Thomas’ answer came a quick exit for Charlie out the back door, a shorter route to the train station, according to Thomas.

It can’t be after 11:15 pm already, Charlie thought. The evening had flown by so quickly; many more questions could have been asked, but he was fascinated with the two business stories he’d heard. Charlie looked back at the town one last time, then stepped up his pace toward the train station. Unsure of what would happen when he got back to the train, he ran back up the stairs to the platform. Out of breath as a man of his age would be, he found Mack standing at the doorway to his railcar, urging him to move quicker.

“Charles, you are late.” Mack was direct and to the point. "Ticket, please."

“But Mack, the instructions said that we needed to be back at 11:15 pm for an 11:30 pm departure. It’s only 11:25 now,” Charlie explained as he tried to catch his breath.

Questioning Mack's authority came with a lesson. "Charles, you are the last one on the train. We were given the okay to leave 10 minutes ago, and I convinced the engineer to hold the train just for you. Next train doesn't come through until tomorrow, and we couldn't have you wandering the streets of Jackson all night, could we?" Mack sounded like a parent, but Charlie was 70 years old. "If you were on Coach Lombardi's team, you were late unless you were 15 minutes early. That is what was called Lombardi Time."

"Yes, I know, Mack. I've used that saying hundreds of times with sales teams and staff. Sometimes, it sank in; other times, it did not. Those that were early were more prepared and ready to make things happen. Three kinds of folks, Mack: Those who make things happen, those who watch things happen, and those who wonder what happened. I always wanted to be the one making it happen."

Mack yelled, "All Aboooard!" He tapped his pocket watch and looked at Charlie. "That was for you, Charles. Let's go!"

CHAPTER 6

Zig Zag

Charlie walked through the dimly lit train car and returned to his seat, only to find a man in a business suit and hat sitting in his seat. "Excuse me, sir, I was sitting here. Not that we can't share the seat, but these are my things and my briefcase above the seat." Charlie had his phone in hand and realized that it was working again.

"Sorry about that. Mind if I join ya?" He spoke with a heavy Southern accent and an oddly familiar pace. "M' name's Art," he said, extending a hand to Charlie. "I'm only travelin' to Yazoo City. Probably could have walked there from Jackson in 'bout the same time with this delay!" Art smiled and continued. "Only 50 miles, but I'd paid my fare already. This here train is pretty much reliable — on schedule, I mean. Back in the day, engineers and conductors wouldn't put up with no delays. Times are different nowadays. I sat on that train platform watching people doin' all sorts of moanin' and groanin', nearly two hours of it."

Charlie was listening with his eyes fixated on Art. "Go on," he encouraged.

"Folks were on their phones, textin' and callin' everyone they knew to tell them how the train done been held up in Jackson, Mississippi, that they ain't got nuthin' to do and that they'd be late to wherever it was they was headin'. Me? I got an hour train ride to Yazoo and got stuck at the station; I had reason to gripe, believe me, but, no sir, not me. Ain't my way."

"Art, I thought you said you were on the platform for two hours, not three?" Charlie was curious about the details.

"I was talking to one lady on the platform. She didn't want to hear nuthin' positive I had to say. I continued on about optimistic people and all their positive energy. She just wanted to wallow in the muck, so to speak. More people like that than ever before, at least that's what I think. So, I decided to board the train early, at about 10:00 pm. Nobody was at the train door, but when I came up them stairs, the conductor grabbed me by the collar and read me the riot act. We had a nice chat about pro-SEED-dure and got that settled quick. Mack's alright, just wanted to make sure I was where I was supposed to be."

"You know Mack?"

"Nope." Art continued. "Just met the big man, him protecting his train, I guess. I showed him my ticket and explained that I just wanted to get on the train early. Tired of that sweltering heat, too. Been a hunerd degrees for the last hunerd days, or so it seems." Art mumbled under his breath, "Global warming."

Charlie tried to get a word in, but it seemed that Art was on a soapbox, "Peoples today, they're in such a hurry, too. Hurry to this, hurry to that. Never seem to be satisfied with where they are. Grew up in Yazoo City. Lived there much of my life before settlin' in Jackson. I've seen much of the world, but I'm happy wherever I am most days."

Art continued. "Heard a travel story about an executive who'd had a long week of business travel. She approached the airport ticket counter where the attendant told her that her flight was canceled. The woman said to the attendant, 'FANTASTIC!'

'Fantastic?' The attendant asked. 'How can a canceled flight be fantastic?' The optimistic woman explained, "There are only three things that would cancel this flight. #1: There's somethin' wrong with the plane. #2: There's somethin' wrong with the weather between here and our destination."

Charlie jumped in, as he had guessed the end of this story. "And #3: There's something wrong with the pilot." He snickered. "I don't want to be on that plane if any of those things are wrong!" Charlie was satisfied with himself for following along.

"You heard that story before, have ya?" Art seemed a bit annoyed that he didn't get to finish the punchline to his story.

"Well, of course I've heard that story before. It's from Zig Ziglar, right?"

Art changed his demeanor immediately, "You know of Zig?" he asked, then realized, "Of course, you do. Everyone our age knew Zig. If you didn't know him, you read his books, listened to his tapes, and learned his many lessons, right?"

"That's right, Art. I was, and still am, a huge fan of Zig Ziglar. I have several of his books and quote stories from him all the time; however, now it seems I have my own stories and experiences to share. Zig was amazing. Saw him speak live in Chicago back when I was just getting started in business, just out of college a few years. He inspired me like no other."

Art continued. "In fact, my nickname is Zag on account I never seemed to run the bases straight. I always got in rundowns, and they started calling me ZigZag. Zag sorta stuck. When I started in business a long time ago, I found out that Zig Ziglar was from my hometown, and his books inspired me from the first time I cracked one open."

"What was your favorite?" asked Charlie.

Art replied without hesitation, "Loved all of them, but *See You at the Top* has gotta be it." Then he realized, "Did they announce Yazoo next?"

The time had flown by with their conversation. "Nope, but Yazoo City shouldn't be far away. What's taking you back home to Yazoo?"

"Funeral in the mornin'. One of my high school baseball teammates died three days ago. Services are tomorra and I wanna pay my respects to the family. I played ball all over and Connolly was one of the best. He's the one who first gave me the Zig-Zag nickname.

Lost touch over the years. Ya get busy, you know? Well, he was a good man. We shoulda talked more or gotten together more — only 40 miles between us — but I guess that happens. I'll see some of my other ol' teammates at the services tomorrow and we'll have a chance to catch up before I head back to Jackson tomorrow night. Catchin' a ride back with one of the guys."

"Ours was obviously NOT a chance meeting, Art," Charlie noted. "Or can I call you Zag?"

"Yes, Zag's fine," Art replied.

"We didn't get to talk baseball, and I'd love to do that with you sometime," Charlie said. "I played adult baseball until I was in my mid 60's. My knees finally did me in since I was a catcher. Baseball is a passion for me. I'm a long time Chicago Cubs fan who grew up going to Wrigley Field at an early age. Celebrated the World Series win back in 2016 in Grant Park and got to see game 7 in Cleveland." He sadly started to get into revved up baseball mode just as his new friend would be getting off the train.

Charlie thought about his experience in Jackson and wondered if, when he got off in Yazoo City, he would go back in time again. The thought was fleeting, and his attention went back to Zag. "Here is my business card. Will you send me your contact information when you can? I would love to get your perspective on other business ideas, Zig Ziglar, and, of course, we can talk baseball all you want."

Zag replied, "You know, I'm a Cub fan, too. We ain't got any major league teams down here. Closest would be in Houston, I reckon. At night or when the radio waves were exactly right, I could get WGN from

Chicago on my transistor radio, even down here in Mississippi. AM 720, ya know?" He knew that he was right. "I loved listening to the play-by-play and the description of Wrigley Field or other ballparks. My dad took me on my first long-distance train ride to Chicago for a weekend series against the Dodgers." He paused as if reminiscing. Then, "Sure, I'll be happy to reach out to you. I give you my word."

"YAZOO CITY! YAZOO CITY, MISSISSIPPI, NEXT!
NEXT STOP, YAZOO CITY, MISSISSIPPI!"

The train was slowing into Yazoo City, and the two knew their time together was ending. Charlie told his new friend, "Some people come into your life for a reason, some for a season, and some for a lifetime. I'm glad that our paths have crossed on this short journey from Jackson. I'm sorry to hear about your friend's passing, and I hope you can find some peace with your teammates tomorrow."

Mack arrived just as the two men were parting. "Looks like the two of you got on pretty well for such a short trip. I thought you might enjoy the company." Mack had a twinkle in his eye as he winked at Zag.

"What do you mean, Mack?" Charlie was insistent.

Zag jumped in, "Well, you see, Charlie, Mack suggested that I sit down here and wait for whoever showed up. Figured it was a sign, and so I just did. I had no idea it would lead to our conversation, but I'm glad it did."

"Mack, so you set this up?"

Mack moved on without saying a word, smiling as he turned toward the doorway. “Yazoo City. Yazoo City arrival!”

Zag clutched Charlie's hand with a firm handshake. "Great to meet you, and I will definitely give you a call next week." He waved the card as if to say, "It’s right here." Zag followed Mack toward the doorway, leaving Charlie alone again.

CHAPTER 7

The Club Car

A voice spoke up near Charlie. "I couldn't help but overhear a bit of your conversation. You're from Chicago, right? Going all the way there?"

Charlie recognized the man who had gotten on at Jackson in the seat in front of him but hadn't noticed anything else about him at the time. Now he noticed he had a young appearance, maybe around 30-35 years old, energetic, and enthusiastic, and he had a look on his face that he'd seen before, a risk-takers eye.

"Yes, I'm going to Chicago." Charlie confirmed, speaking softly in the dimly lit train car, as onboarding passengers had started to settle in for some sleep.

"I'm going home to Chicago, too," the young man said in a whisper. "I heard that there's an overnight card game up in the Club Car. You up for joining me?"

Charlie yawned as he looked at his phone. It was 12:30 am, but he appreciated this young man's kind invitation. "I'll go with you for a while. I'm getting kind of tired."

Just then, Mack tapped them each on the shoulder and said, "Excuse me, gentleman, I wanted the two of you to know that a sleeping berth has become available. A passenger needed to get off the train in Yazoo City for medical reasons, and her berth is now empty." He added, "Thanks for keeping it down. Others are trying to sleep."

Charlie tried to be gracious, "He can take it. I don't sleep much anyway and was planning to wake up to the sunrise out my window here."

The man graciously declined. "I'm heading to the Club Car for a night of cards. Don't need no sleeper. You take it."

Mack took over the conversation authoritatively, "Charles, the berth is #6 in car #6 just behind the Sightseer Car. It has a 'just cleaned' sticker across the handle, and the doors are wide open with the lower bed already made up. You, sir, should be wary of that card game, if you know what I mean. It isn't for amateurs," he said with the tone of a parent warning his kid about the dangers of playing with matches. "Make sure you know when to hold them and know when to fold them." He had that smile again as he turned to walk away.

Charlie quietly called after him in his best Kenny Roger's impersonation, "Are we on a train bound for nowhere?" He smiled at his own wittiness.

"Karaoke takes place in the Parlour Car on the southbound trip, Charles." Mack joked as he used the formal name of the club car. "The staff members in the dining car said that your voice is exceptional. However, it's late, and the other passengers aren't interested in hearing you."

Both men got up to follow the conductor. Mack led the two of them from car to car, trying to be quiet with each door opening between cars. The night air was still moist in between cars, and the noise of the train rumbling was coupled with the silence of each car they passed through.

Once they got to the dining car, which was now closed and empty, Mack spoke in a normal tone of voice. "Breakfast will be available beginning at 6:30 am, no sooner. We hope to be in Memphis by then. We'll have a brief stop there to load some freight, and that's where we get our fuel. It's our heaviest passenger load stop, and you will be able to get off the train as you did in Jackson, with the same restrictions as before; you must have your boarding pass to get back on the train. And you, Charles, you better be on Lombardi time!" Mack pointed at him directly, smiling while doing so.

"Yes sir," both men said, giving their best military salutes as Mack headed back toward his passenger cars. The two men continued forward to the Club Car.

"My name's Charlie; I didn't get yours." Jazz music played softly in the background as they entered the Club Car.

"The name's Quick James Quick. Most people call me Jimmy. I'm a trader at the Board of Trade; moved to Chicago about four years ago from New York. Lost my job on the New York Stock Exchange and had a friend in Chicago who said I should come out there to work. I struggled to find a job and mounted up some credit card debt, but I have it under control. I have been working at the Board for about a year now, and they give me lots of PTO. Took the train to New Orleans a week ago and been gamblin' down there. I took a cash advance in Jackson when we stopped."

Jimmy's eyes lit up as he saw the big poker game at the far end of the car.

"Wait a minute," Charlie started to ask the young man, "You've been on the train since New Orleans, got off in Jackson, found an ATM, and got back on the train? Did you see anything unusual about Jackson?"

The man tilted his head questioningly at Charlie. "Nope, nothing except the ATM at the station wasn't working. I had to go looking for the closest bank. I found a drive-through ATM, and I felt a little odd walking up to it with a car waiting behind me." Jimmy recalled it as though it had just happened, though it had been a couple of hours ago. "I nodded off for a bit while we waited for the tracks to be cleared, other than that, nothing odd has happened so far this trip."

Charlie left it at that and didn't pursue why or how he had seen what he'd seen at the hotel and hardware store.

"You think you'll win big tonight?" Charlie was curious about Jimmy's approach and confidence.

"Of course, I'm going to win big; why would I think otherwise?" He was confident. "Made millions for my clients over the years by taking a risk. Of course, I've had my share of losses, too. Made some deals that didn't work out but learned some things as well. Comme si, Comme sa."

"Have a family?" Charlie picked up on Jimmy's words 'over the years' thinking he may be older than he looked.

Jimmy avoided the question, clearly uninterested in small talk, as the two moved closer to the crowded table. Jimmy ensured the players knew he was interested in the next chair that opened up.

"Likely cash only," Charlie warned his new friend. And by the looks of some of the men there, a serious bit of it is at stake. Are you sure you want to get in on this?" Charlie's caution sounded much like Mack's a few minutes earlier. "If you get in the game, I'll watch you for a few minutes. Otherwise, I'm going to get some shut eye. It's getting late, and I have a bed waiting for me in berth #6." Charlie allowed himself a big but quiet yawn.

Jimmy's shoulder got tapped by the man who'd just gone all in and lost with pocket eights. "Your turn, buddy. I hope your luck is better than mine was. Brutal. Cards didn't seem to come all night."

Jimmy turned to Charlie. "Thanks for the chat, Mack, I mean Charlie. #6 is my lucky number. Do you mind if I use the sleeping bunk in the morning? AFTER you get up, that is." They both laughed.

"Nope, I don't sleep much anyway," Charlie replied. "I'll make sure to tell Mack that we'll be sharing the sleeping berth so that someone doesn't wake you later on. Good luck and remember to know when to fold them."

Charlie's song reference went in one ear and out the other; Jimmy's mind was already on the game.

Charlie watched the first couple of hands and could see that Jimmy was intense. He had played cards himself over the years and understood the strategy all too well. The adrenaline rush that comes from gambling feeds the continuation of it. One lost hand is met by the anticipation of that next winning jackpot. Charlie had overcome the urge to play all night, recognizing that it would be easy for him to fall into that desire again.

Charlie moved from the club car and then through the Sightseer observation car for the first time. The curved glass ceiling and floor-to-ceiling windows had only the darkness to show this late at night. Blue lights gave it a quiet feel, and one man lay in a fetal position on one of the couches. He was obviously trying to get some sleep. As Charlie entered the sleeping car, each compartment was clearly marked with numbers. All of them had their blinds drawn; #6 was on the left and just as Mack had described, bed made and ready to crawl in. As he settled into his compartment, he heard the loudspeaker.

"GREENWOOD! GREENWOOD, MISSISSIPPI, NEXT!
NEXT STOP, GREENWOOD, MISSISSIPPI!"

CHAPTER 8

If God Gave You Thirty Hours, Would You Still Sleep Six?

Charlie had looked at his cell phone before closing his eyes, noting that it was 1:15 am. He recalled the train slowing down and thought he remembered that the train had stopped, but maybe not before he fell fast asleep. Stops and starts had become regular occurrences as part of the trip. Dozing off was easy for Charlie once he was tired.

Upon waking the next morning, Charlie slowly moved his limbs as his body came to life. *Stiff, but not as stiff as I would have been sleeping upright in coach or curled up on that couch. I'll have to remember to thank Mack,* he thought.

Charlie made some mental notes as he started each day. *What time is it?* Charlie reached over the thin cotton sheet to the ledge where his cell sat dimly lit in its night mode. *6:05 am? Can't be,* he thought to himself. But he knew better. He had been diagnosed with Short Sleepers Syndrome in his late 50s. This gene mutation (DEC2 and ABRD1), which has been studied extensively at the University of California San Fransisco, affected his body's need for sleep, meaning he could get away with six, five, or even four hours of sleep without any adverse effects. It was both a blessing and a curse, he knew.

Charlie was generally cheerful and optimistic. Most days, he didn't need a nap and never drank coffee or Mt Dew to keep himself awake. Most importantly, he didn't need to catch up on his sleep on the weekend, even when he had no reason otherwise to be up early. In his early adulthood, Charlie was tagged as a workaholic, which he agreed he probably was. But the Short Sleeper's diagnosis was a game changer. After having some angst about the diagnosis, Charlie embraced and leaned into the nuances associated with the disorder rather than looking for clues on how to solve it.

Most recently, the early morning hours grew earlier. With only a few hours of sleep, it meant limited options existed. Charlie could either lie in bed thinking about the day or quietly get up and read, type, work, or meditate quietly on the couch as he often did. With the recent creation of his new book outline, online research was time-consuming, but what else did he have to do? His body clock seemed to wake him long before others even dreamed of their alarms going off.

Most often, Charlie found a way to be productive and embraced his situation rather than whining about it. Instead, he wrote articles and outlined his day. He sent emails that would be received hours later because he used the scheduling tool within Outlook, so it might appear that the email was sent at 8:30 am rather than at 4:30 am. (Charlie loved that functionality.)

Charlie had calculated what an extra two waking hours per day might yield in productivity. It meant that over 18 extra 40-hour weeks were available to him in two-hour, bite-sized pieces. Who wouldn't like to have over 700 additional hours a year at their disposal? The reality was that Charlie had no control over the situation. He never set an alarm; he slept when tired and woke up refreshed every day. Not everyone could do that, and Charlie understood that. He cautioned his friends to make sure to see their own physician or have a study done about their own sleep challenges because the risks of adverse health issues were genuine.

What the condition meant, unlike overtime on a job where hours get recorded and compensated for, was that he had the time to plan business strategies and execute those plans differently than other business professionals. Lately, Charlie had become obsessed with the hypothetical question: "If God gave you 30 hours per day, would you still sleep six?" and he started many conversations with it. The concept intrigued most people he talked with.

Some people said that if given an extra six hours, they'd sleep it away, or that they may be even more productive. Others said they would spend the extra hours with their family, giving them more quality time than they might have otherwise. Still others took a hybrid approach and told Charlie they'd sleep two more hours, work two more, and play or have family time with the other two.

Some people asked Charlie what God had to do with it. Why would God give us an additional six hours? After all, the day is only 24 hours long, with two 12-hour periods sandwiched by noon and midnight, regardless of the time zone, across the planet.

Charlie always had the same answer regarding God's involvement in the hypothetical. "Who would have the power to give you six more hours in a day? The only answer is God, right? He is an almighty, powerful, and loving God. Who else could grant such a thing?"

Charlie had stayed up 30 hours straight more than once without any sleep; he knew other business owners who had business challenges that kept them up at night, too. His were often anxiety-filled, with business or personal challenges that, at times, brought him to tears. It was cliché for consultants to ask, "What keeps you up at night?" However, business leaders are less than honest with their responses because they are too proud to admit they need help.

"MEMPHIS! MEMPHIS, TENNESSEE, NEXT! NEXT STOP, MEMPHIS, TENNESSEE!"

Had he not heard other stops through the night? Did he sleep that soundly? Charlie thought about how much he hated waking to an alarm. He rarely set one due to his Short Sleepers Syndrome. He'd be up before the alarm, even on travel days when he needed to be at the airport by 5:00 am; today was no different.

Everyone knew that Charlie was an early riser. His former colleagues, Harlan and Quinn, were among a handful of people who could call before 7:00 am, knowing that he would be up. (*I'll have to write that down somewhere for safekeeping,* Charlie thought with a smirk on his face. *Harlan-Quinn...maybe I'll make my next business book a romance novel instead.*

Charlie sat up on the bed and peeked out the window at the spectacular sunrise. *Beautiful,* he thought. He took a picture of the morning landscape with his cell phone.

Then...*Rita!* He startled himself, wondering if he'd forgotten to text her or if she had tried to text him. Checking his phone, he saw his message from the day before:

3:45 pm – Hey Babe. Change in plans. Taking the train to Chicago rather than flying. All other plans are the same. Call when you want. I'll be traveling for 20 hours. The train is due tomorrow morning around noon.

Rita's missed replies followed.

5:45 pm – Closing today, on a break. Will call you later. Dogs are outside, and all is good here. Enjoy your train ride. Love you.

7:58 pm – Sorry, forgot to call. I took the dogs for a walk and am here if you want to talk. Love you.

9:02 pm – You likely got caught up in a conversation on the train, have bad service, or are asleep in your seat. I'm going to bed early and will talk to you in the morning. Sleep well.

Charlie considered what his morning text would be and was certainly not going to summarize everything that had happened on his rail adventure.

6:22 am – Good morning, Babe. Hope you slept well. Somehow missed your texts from last night. I'll be up two hours by the time you get this. Fantastic train ride, and too many things to share by text. Some experiences I am unsure that I can even explain. Weird. Outrageous. God is on board the train, and it has been magical. The train is way late, and we aren't likely to get into Chicago until late this afternoon or early evening. Will call from Chicago once I'm settled into my hotel. Love you MORE! Hugs from outside of Memphis.

Charlie reread the message before hitting send and added a kiss emoji to seal the deal. *We still think of ourselves as newlyweds,* he thought to himself as he tried to justify his playful nature. Charlie knew in his heart that Rita and he had to work hard to keep that fire going between them. He thought about holding hands with her in the car or as they walked. The smack on the butt she would give him as he pulled something from the bottom shelf of the refrigerator. The early morning snuggle time was intentional because they didn't have the energy for lovemaking at the end of a long day at their older age. He realized he was fantasizing about her when the sound of approaching footsteps stopped outside his door. Then a thud came from the other side.

He got up to investigate and opened the compartment door. "Jimmy! you look awful, buddy, if you don't mind me saying so."

Jimmy was wearing the same clothes as the night before. His shirt was untucked, several buttons were undone, and his eyes were bloodshot. The smell of alcohol was on his breath, but Charlie didn't give it much thought. "Card game didn't go so well, eh?"

"I don't want to talk about it," the young man mumbled. "I just want to sleep it off. Hoped you were done in #6 and that I could crash. I can come back later."

Assessing the situation, Charlie quickly replied, "No, just give me a minute to collect my things, and you can have the bed. You certainly need it more than me." He pulled his loafers onto his feet, made sure that his few things went with him, and fluffed the pillows, making it easy for Jimmy to get into the bed.

"Jimmy, the place is all yours. Here is a fresh blanket." He smiled knowingly at the young man as they awkwardly passed each other in the doorway.

"Charlie, thank you for sharing your bed with me." It came out in a humorous way that Jimmy hadn't intended. “Well, you know what I mean,” he said sheepishly.

“Sure, Jimmy. You’ll feel better after a few hours of sleep,” Charlie encouraged. “You know where you can find me when you wake up. Second car from the engine. I am not going anywhere this train doesn’t go.”

Charlie moved forward into the observation car and took a seat all alone. As he did, he caught glimpses of the rural landscape out the spacious windows. Before long, the view became a modern city, with the sun glistening off the mirrored windows of skyscrapers. The train soon slowed to a more moderate pace. Entering the city, he heard the long-long-short-long train whistle more often as the locomotive passed many crossings.

Charlie stood up and started toward the front of the train. When he arrived at the dining car, he saw it had been set up with bagels, donuts, fruit, and juice…buffet style.

The attendant encouraged Charlie to take a plate. “Help yourself, sir, unless you’d like to sit down and order.”

“I think I will just take something to go,” Charlie replied. He grabbed a glass of orange juice and chose a chocolate-covered donut. "Breakfast of Champions!" he said to the attendant with a smile.

Charlie moved on through the passenger cars one by one, trying not to spill his juice as he passed between each one. It was obviously another humid summer day in the South. The haze was already looming, and it wasn’t even 7:00 am yet.

CHAPTER 9

Memphis Grand Central Station

Charlie returned to his seat just as Mack came through the car with a travel update. "Our brief stop, Charles, will be exactly 60 minutes, no more, no less. If you intend to get off the train to explore Memphis, I suggest you forego breakfast at one of the area diners." Noticing his donut, he added, "Looks like you have a snack to get you started anyway."

Charlie took a bite and said, "As you can see," rubbing his belly with a jolly laugh, "my money has been invested in Dunkin' for a long time." Changing to a more serious tone, he warned, "Mack, you might not want to disturb my friend Jimmy. He's asleep in berth #6; we swapped places a few minutes ago. I think he had a rough night at the card table."

"No need to explain, Charles," Mack spoke with a directness that Charlie was beginning to know him for. "I passed through the club car on my 5:00 am rounds. Only the heavy hitters were left, including, of course, young Mr. Quick. His chips were about gone, and I expect he'd reached into his pockets one too many times." Mack continued, "I've heard many stories from people on the train about making money quick and losing it even quicker in their business endeavors...far faster at the gaming tables from what I've seen. We'll let Mr. Quick sleep, and I'll check on him after a while. We still have over 12 hours to Chicago. We are usually on time; most we're ever delayed is a couple of hours."

"Twelve hours?" Charlie asked. "With this Memphis stop, do you have a new ETA?"

"Well, if I were a betting man, and I am not," Mack looked at his pocket watch with that gleam in his eye that Charlie had seen before, "I'd say that we'll be pulling into Chicago's Union Station at 8:35 pm this evening. I may be off by a bit, but that's the best guess I have for you at this point."

"8:35 pm, that's a pretty precise answer," Charlie challenged Mack's response. "Willing to back that up with a $1.00 bet?"

"Charles, a friendly wager I will take. Neither of us is going broke on $1.00. Want to make it another dollar and bet on the Cubs or White Sox winning another World Series this Fall?" Now Mack was starting to play with Charlie by poking fun at the losing baseball teams.

Mack pulled out a Morgan silver dollar from his pocket with the year 1889 minted into it. "Tell you what, if I'm off by more than five minutes of our arrival in Union Station, you can keep my special coin. Otherwise, you'll have to return it to me with a $1.00 of your own. Deal?"

The two shook on it, and Charlie put the coin in his back left pocket for safekeeping just as the train pulled to a stop.

"Now remember Charles," Mack looked at his pocket watch again, "We're pulling out of Memphis at 8:00 am *sharp*, with or without you. I hope you enjoy the beautiful new Memphis Grand Central Station. If you have time, check out the Memphis Union Station, too. It's just to the east."

"Yes sir, Mr. Lombardi sir," Charlie joked. "I'll be back in 45 minutes." Charlie stood up straight as if the coach were talking to the whole team. "By the way, how will *your* Packers do against *my* Bears this Fall?"

The two laughed as they parted, and Mack went to take his post at the exit doors and help other passengers on and off.

Charlie looked at his phone to see if Rita had responded to his text yet, but she hadn't. He thought to himself, *probably still asleep as she usually would be at this time of the morning*.

A confirming email from the manager at the Hyatt Regency O'Hare informed Charlie that his reservation for last night had been canceled and that he would be moved to the downtown riverfront Hyatt Regency in Chicago for the next two nights. Earlier in his career, Charlie had provided a series of referrals to both Chicago properties, helping them book various lucrative conferences. It seemed this favor meant that they were accommodating him with a suite upgrade.

The email ended with, “Thank you for trusting your stay with us. We’ll see you later this evening.” That was personal service — something very precious today.

Charlie stepped off the train to the platform, and again, he noticed that he was likely the last passenger to leave the train. He walked into the station through the large cast iron doors and down the steps. He found the station deserted; Charlie scratched his head. Looking around the station, everything looked old but fresh in a magnificent way. Mack had told him to enjoy the station's beauty, though he didn’t know what that meant at the time.

An approaching woman caught Charlie’s attention. Charlie appeared to be out of place as far as she was concerned since the station wasn’t supposed to be open yet.

“May I help you sir?” she asked. The woman looked to be in her thirties, had a slight tear in her trouser knee, hair under her baseball cap, and wore a manly work shirt.

"Well, maybe." Charlie felt odd, similar to his experience in Jackson, Mississippi, just last evening.

"It has been an odd couple of days, and I don't know if I can explain it fully. I just got off the morning train."

The woman interrupted, "But how'd you get in here? Doors 'been locked and nobody's supposed to be in here until the ribbon cutting in October. Passengers are supposed to be outside; the stairs to town are at the end of the platform. I'm afraid I'll have to ask you to leave."

"Just a minute, you say all the other passengers are outside the station?" Charlie was curious about where everyone from the train had gone.

"Yes, sir. This station is set to open on October 4th with all sorts of new services. And yes, we'll have indoor toilets," the woman bragged.

"I'm Rosie, in charge of maintenance and such here at the Memphis Grand Central Station, not to be confused with the Union Station. If you'd like to talk to the station manager, I can get him for you. If you want to know anything about this building or the railroad, he's your man. I was hired to take care of the place."

"Yes, I think I'd like that. Where might I find him?" Charlie asked, hearing his voice echo through the cavernous hall.

"You wait right here. Don't go wandering off; Mr. Presley wouldn't like that." Rosie headed off through the large hall, and Charlie stayed put as Rosie had suggested. He spun around slowly to check out the amazing structure, noticing the massive amount of seating for so many travelers. As he noticed the restroom signs, he wandered in that direction, forgetting his promise to Rosie. As he grew near, the hair on his arms stood on end.

"Whites ONLY," the sign read.

While he knew there were places in the South that still held segregationist ideas today, he was confident that a large city like Memphis was not that place. Charlie looked closer at the hand-made sign, which was still wet, like it had just been painted.

Heavy footsteps right behind him made Charlie turn to see that, indeed, Mr. Presley was approaching.

“I'm Mr. Presley, the station master. Miss Cartwright said that you wanted to see me. You have some questions about our train station?"

Mr. Presley was dressed nicely but in work clothes, more put together than Rosie. His pressed shirt could have been worn with a suit, and his black shoes were spit-shined. Charlie often noticed these kinds of details to assess how to break the ice with someone. Clearly the Whites ONLY sign had caught him off guard.

“Hello, Mr. Presley. My name is Charlie, and I’m on my way from New Orleans to Chicago. The train stopped to pick up some freight and passengers traveling north from Memphis.”

“Yes, sir.” Presley listened attentively.

“I got off the train and wandered into the station; came through those doors right over there.” Charlie pointed to the doors facing the tracks.

Presley nodded in acknowledgment. “I’ve told our crews that they are to keep those doors locked at all times. But now that you’re here, what can I do for you?”

Charlie started again. “I’m just confused because so many things I’m seeing and hearing just don't add up." He looked at his phone to see how much time he had remaining, but the phone was dead again. "What time do you have?" He looked up and saw a large clock on the wall; it said 7:20. "Oh, I see now. Apparently, it's 7:20 am. Just to confirm, I'm in Memphis Grand Central Station. I guess not to be confused with the Union Station?"

"That is correct, and yes, by my account, it is, in fact, 7:20 am. If it were PM, we'd have the sunlight coming in those windows instead of these." Presley pointed in both directions with a repressed irritation in his voice at the obvious nature of his statement. "We are scheduled to open up this station in just three months. It is far nicer than the old station which had been on this site. We are hosting a grand party in October. Hoping President Wilson will come through on the train to usher it in!"

"President Wilson? What year is this?" Charlie was astonished but was just now beginning to put the clues together.

"This is 1914, and the city is getting ready to celebrate Independence Day; the Fourth of July is coming up next week."

"You don't say," Charlie chuckled to himself, knowing what he'd experienced the night before in Jackson.

"We throw a real humdinger of a celebration here in Memphis!" Then, noticing the ashen look on Charlie's face, he asked, "Would you like to sit down? You appear weak in the knees, Mister. What did you say your name was?"

"Charlie, Sir, and yes, I'd appreciate that. I have some questions that I think you can clear up for me."

The two moved to the seating area and sat beside one another, looking out into the grand hall.

"You may not believe this, but by my calendar, this isn't 1914 at all." Charlie hesitated to get the words right but realized there was no such thing, so he continued. "It appears that I've traveled by train into the past and have somehow found this old... well... NEW train station."

"You don't say?" Presley looked confused.

"Yes, something similar happened to me in Jackson, Mississippi, last evening. I met people from 1914, and we had some very nice conversations about doing business, then and now." Charlie was trying to choose his words so as not to seem psychotic to the station master. "You see, I'm not sure why any of this is happening to me, but it must be a magical year because of a book I've written about this time period."

"Well, Charlie, I'm not sure what's going on with you, but it sure is special for us here at the Grand Central Station with the official opening and all. That likely isn't what you're talking about though."

Presley continued, "Nearly 50 years since the War for Southern Independence took place, and folks in these parts may not be up to celebrating, but 50's a round number anyway. Nothing was civil about the War Between the States — brothers against brothers, family against family. My pappy fought in the war and didn't return home. My mama raised us kids, but then she died also, so my sisters raised me through my teenage years. I hope we never have to go through another war again; I turn 55 next month."

Clearly, Presley felt comfortable talking with Charlie but was skeptical as well as curious. "You say that you come from the future, is that right? Do we have wars between now and then?"

Charlie could go on for days talking of WWII, Korea, Vietnam, and all the wars leading up to the Gulf War and the most recent conflicts around the world. Not to mention that WWI was on the brink of erupting within that month.

"Let's leave the answer as 'Yes' for simplicity. I could tell you much of what will happen in the coming years, but that would be unfair to you and those you would share it with," Charlie decided.

Charlie chuckled to himself because if Presley had a Gmail account, they could correspond back and forth across time.

Overwhelmed with this idea of time travel, Presley changed the subject. "What do you do for a living, Charlie? Do you go around inspecting new train stations?" Presley winked at his own joke.

Chuckling, Charlie replied, "Not at all. I have been in sales and leadership roles for nearly 50 years. When I first started in business after graduating college, I was a traveling salesman like my grandfather. He sold caskets. Everyone travels from place to place in cars. In fact, in the future, people will travel in large airplanes that fly at hundreds of miles per hour. In the 21st century, an airplane ride from New Orleans to Chicago is less than three hours. I am taking the train only because, well...never mind that. In my world, trains aren't as popular as they are in yours, Mr. Presley. I am, however, really enjoying my time riding the train, and, like I said, I should be in Chicago later tonight."

“Well, Charlie, we get all sorts of salesmen coming through our station — the old station, that is. They come with a trunkful of items they’re trying to pedal to our local shop owners. They move from one town to the next, stay in our hotels, eat our food, and move on to the next town. Some salesmen stay in Memphis all week, set up their products in a nearby hotel and the shop owners come there to see what kind of new products they have. Innovating things, too, believe me. I’ve seen them talking to one another as they wait for the next train. They share their stories and pass on names of new shop owners or buyers.”

Charlie jumped in, "Those are called referrals," he was in his element again. "I have studied how business is done in 1914, and it is fascinating. It’s not a whole lot different than we do in my era, but we have more advanced technology.”

“Tech-what?” Presley was engaged but had never heard that word before.

Charlie pulled out his phone and showed Presley the blank screen as he’d done with Julius the evening before. “In my day, we use this machine for everything. It’s a personal telephone, our source of information and communication, all in one little machine. It isn't working, I guess, because the satellites aren't in the sky yet."

Clearly, his response went over Presley’s head. “We’ve got three telephones in this whole building. Don’t need more than that, on account of not many people having them in their businesses or homes. They’re becoming more widely used, more so than telegraph. We still use the telegraph between our stations on the line. Helps to know when the train's going to be late."

"Telegraph is a thing of the past where I come from. Everyone will have a telephone; even young children will carry one in their pocket. Yes, they will." Charlie forgot that he didn't want to foreshadow too much of the future.

Wanting to still learn more before departing, Charlie said, "I must leave in a moment, but I have a couple more questions before I do. First of all, there is a 'Whites ONLY' sign outside your restrooms. Where do the Black people go? Also, Rosie, Miss Cartright, she's in charge? I would have thought that in 1914, a man would be in charge of maintenance in a place as large as this. Can you tell me about these things?"

Presley leaned in toward Charlie and grabbed his hand. "See these hands of yours? They're white. Mine, too. The law says no Black people can use the toilets here. It's a shame." His tone was soft, knowing that his voice could be heard throughout the grand hall, but nobody else was in the building at that hour. "They gotta go just the same as you and I. Fifty years ago, we heard Mr. Lincoln say people's the same, but we have not done enough to see it through, at least as far as I'm concerned. We still got a long way to go."

"As for Miss Cartright, she's the hardest working person I know. She outworks 20 men most days. It comes natural for her. You see, her father taught her everything he knew. He helped her into a job or two. She worked for nothing in some instances to show the boss she could do the job as well as or better than anyone else. She doesn't have any children to care for at home, either. Here in 1914, most women her age are at home taking care of children, have got a maid doing the housework, and have a paid boy taking care of the rose garden. The way I see it, Rosie needs to support herself. I have just given her the chance to do it when others haven't."

So ended the lesson from Presley.

"My oh my, Mr. Presley, you sure know how to make a difference. I'm sure you will do your best to help those with different skin colors get ahead when possible. Hopefully, you will pass that passion along to your kids and to your grandkids when you have them."

"Got my first grandbaby coming around Christmas time. A blessing for sure." Presley was obviously proud.

"I must be on my way, Mr. Presley, but I appreciate your hospitality and perspective. I sure hope that President Wilson makes his way to Memphis for your upcoming grand opening. You have a beautiful train station and a wonderful outlook. May I shake your hand?"

As the two stood up, Presley firmly gripped Charlie's hand. "God bless you and thank you for visiting Memphis. You are welcome back anytime." As Charlie headed up the stairs, Presley shouted, "You're going the wrong way if you want to see the Union Station; it's to the east, a couple of blocks from here."

Charlie knew that he didn't have enough time before he had to be back on the train. "Next time! Thank you. Thank you very much." Charlie waved as if he was walking off a rock and roll concert stage. He swiveled his hips and smiled as he pushed through the cast-iron doors back onto the platform.

Chapter 10

Mending Fences

Charlie arrived back to the train at precisely 7:45 am. He was greeted at the door by Mack, who asked for Charlie's ticket. He reached into his back left pocket, but the only thing there was Mack's silver dollar. "Mack, I must have left it with my other things on my seat. You know who I am; you gave me this coin just an hour ago."

Mack shared another lesson, "You know the rules, Charles. You must have your ticket with you at all times. How else can we keep order on the train? What if another conductor was here and not me? What would you do then?"

"I would ask for a bit of grace, a few minutes to run to my seat and produce the ticket. Could you give me that grace, Mack?" He thought Mack would let him pass, but again, Mack decided to leave Charlie to squirm in the warm Southern air.

"I would like to ask you a question, Charles. Do you grant employees or family members grace when they ask for it? All the time? Be honest now." Mack was being harsh.

"You know Mack, no, I haven't always. I try my best, but sometimes a lesson has to be taught." Charlie caught himself in his own words.

"You want to repeat that for yourself, Charles, or would you like me to repeat it for you?"

Charlie understood that if he could choose when to grant a favor or grace, certainly Mack had the same right to do so. He smiled to himself as he recognized the reminder and coincidental reference to Grace in the land of Graceland and Elvis. After all, he'd just met a man named Presley.

"You win, Mack. Would you like your silver dollar back? Will that get me back on the train?"

"No, Charles, you can't buy your way back in. That's not how it works, and you, of all people, should know that."

Charlie felt scolded.

Mack lightened up. "Come on, get on board. We are heading out of here. We must get you up to Chicago by nightfall, right? All Aboooard!" Mack shouted as loud as he could. "That's for you, Charles!"

As the train chugged down the track, Charlie watched the Grand Central Station become smaller and smaller. He saw the Union Station that both Presley and Mack had talked about. Two train stations in Memphis seemed odd to Charlie, but he would have to look into that later. What was a vast, colossal train depot just a few minutes earlier was reduced to a tiny spot in the distant landscape of this modern city. Charlie marveled at the experience, his conversations, and his brief passage back to 1914. It felt like a gift.

The train appeared to be going faster than it otherwise had been during the trip. Charlie imagined that the engineer was trying to make up time. Infrastructure changes on the tracks took place years earlier with investment in high-speed rail segments.

Charlie sat in his seat, reminiscing about the last transformational 24 hours and how different Jackson and Memphis were in 1914. He thought about the people he'd met, tried to put himself in their shoes, and imagined himself living at that time. The trees and fields flew past at an unbelievable rate of speed, almost a blur as he looked out on the Tennessee morning sky. *Not unlike our lives here on earth*, Charlie thought to himself. He wasn't a young man any longer, and his years were numbered, but he knew that only God knew when his time on earth would be complete. He repeatedly told others, "Tomorrow is promised to no one."

Charlie reflected on his life, and it was good. He'd experienced sadness and challenges. If just one thing had changed during his childhood, Charlie realized, his life could have gone in so many different directions. He had gone to five different schools before he had gotten to junior high — three for third grade alone. He was a product of divorce and a true latch-key kid. Charlie thought about the adults who shaped and protected him, sometimes just from himself and the stupid things teenagers do.

He thought about Andy Rasch, owner of Rasch Pharmacy, where Charlie worked throughout high school. Andy was a character, the kind that a teenager respected but didn't really understand. Charlie often shared the humorous Rasch Pharmacy motto: "We're itching to serve you." It was Andy's chance to be clever.

Charlie remembered a closing-time conver-sation with his boss. "Son," Andy said, "You'll know when you meet that right woman. You'll know it. You'll get married, have some kids, and before you realize it, you'll be sitting there on the toilet doing your business, and she'll be at the makeup counter getting ready to go out."

Charlie hadn't thought about that story for a long time. He smiled and saw his aging face in the train window reflection. It stood still as the landscape flew past behind him.

Charlie recognized that his first marriage was rooted in youthful love and friendship. He often said that he married his best friend. They shared a love of sports, old movies, and family values. They started dating in college and married after graduation. With the job changes, moves from one house to the next, three exceptional children, and a lengthy career in sales, Charlie yearned to own his own business. It was a challenge that demanded his time, which he tried to balance with his personal life.

Charlie recalled all the time and energy that he'd invested in building business relationships. His teams appreciated his honest and caring approach to leadership, and his clients found him to be resourceful on their behalf. Charlie remembered how important it was to take care of repeat customers as much as it was to generate new ones. This led him to valuable business friendships with longtime clients and past employees.

Charlie thought about his life as the train rushed down the tracks. He remembered parties, funerals, vacations, and new cars. Specific customers and sales situations passed through his memory, but as quickly as they came to mind, he was on to the next recollection. Dates and years stood out and mounted like stacks of coins that Charlie had placed on his dresser. Coins reminded him of his coin-snatching trick and a whirlwind trip to Hollywood. The thought of Hollywood led him to all of his trips to California over the years, which in turn had him thinking about all of his travels. Charlie marveled that Alaska was the only state he hadn't traveled to in his 70 years; however, he was going on a summer Alaskan cruise with the kids and grandkids in September.

Charlie's eyelids were heavy. He felt like he did when driving in a rain or snowstorm with windshield wipers hypnotically putting him to sleep. This time he wasn't behind the wheel, and he dozed off.

"FULTON! FULTON, KENTUCKY, NEXT!
NEXT STOP, FULTON, KENTUCKY!"

Charlie awoke to the sound of the train announcement and a young woman standing in the aisle next to his seat. She had pink hair and appeared to be in her early 20s.

"You don't know how far we are from Fulton, do you? They just made the announcement, and I know that we're late," she said as she sat in the seat on the opposite side of the aisle from Charlie. Then, absentmindedly, she muttered, "I haven't been able to text my friend and hope that she'll be there to meet me."

"No, I don't know what time we're supposed to be anywhere. The schedule is way off-kilter. Mack, the conductor, may be around. He would know for sure. It shouldn't be long after the speaker's announcement; it seems to be only a few minutes before we get to our next stop." He offered his name first. "Hi, I'm Charlie."

"Hi. I'm Priscilla." She then added, somewhat self-consciously, "After Elvis' daughter. My mom worship-ped Elvis."

Charlie thought to himself, *can this get any odder?* But as with all things, he leaned into it. "Nice to meet you, Priscilla. I just met a man in Memphis by the name of Presley!" Priscilla didn't seem to care.

The train began to slow down, but they were still in the country. Corn and soybeans lined both sides of the track, and pastures went on for miles in the rolling hills of Western Kentucky.

"We seem to be stopping, but I don't think we're in a town," Charlie looked out the window and could clearly see they were not at a station. "Mack, you're just in time."

"Always am." He winked. "Can't stay. Cows."

"Cows?" Charlie asked, shrugging his shoulders.

"Yes, we were making good time," Mack started. "Making up time, as a matter of fact, nothing between stations to keep our engineer pushing the engine to its maximum speed. We got a report that cattle were on the tracks and had to slow down to ensure we didn't plow through them. Wouldn't be good for us or the cattle."

Mack continued hurriedly. "Fences are hard to keep mended in these parts. Cows roaming off of property onto our tracks. It causes delays for us, and each time we talk about mending fences to the farmers, they tell us the same thing. 'Hard to mend fences.' But we keep trying. I'll be back through this way when I can, but this is obviously another setback to our schedule."

As Mack continued towards the front of the train, Priscilla spoke to Charlie. "Mister, I need to try to text my friend again. While it's nice to talk with you, I need some space, please."

The young woman turned her back to Charlie, looked out the window, searched for the cows, and texted on her phone.

Charlie thought about what Mack had said about mending fences. This immediately brought him to tears. As had happened just a while ago, his mind flashed to all his missteps over the years. People he had offended or situations that needed care and tending.

Family issues came to mind, one after another. *How could all of those fences be mended?* he wondered. Some were easily fixed, and others were not. You can't choose your children or your parents. He had said that to business friends over the years and tried to share his family story when he could. Sharing a burden can be helpful to both the person with the challenge, as well as the person who's willing to listen.

He admitted to himself that there were some business relationships he didn't want to be mended. He recalled a lawsuit that caused him a lot of pain. He'd forgiven the person bringing the suit but didn't forget. He had bosses that were less than perfect, but neither was he. After all, the only perfect person walked the earth over 2000 years ago.

Now, Mack, Charlie thought to himself, *he's a solid guy with his head on straight. I'll have to stay in touch with him.*

Charlie wondered why the cows had stopped this particular train on this particular day, at this specific time. *Couldn't it have occurred five minutes later? We'd have been traveling at break-neck speed without a stop.* The thought was fleeting, but Charlie already knew the answer to that one. Nothing is random; everything has a reason. *Maybe we were supposed to learn that our world is moving too fast sometimes and that we need to slow down.* Certainly, Charlie could use that reminder. His mind wandered back to the mending of fences comment that Mack had made.

We have to keep mending fences; I think that's what he said. If that's how he put it, he is spot-on. I can't count how many times I've had to say I'm sorry over a lifetime; must be thousands, he thought. How many times did he need forgiveness, and were others so willing to forgive? Some offenses hurt, and some wounds were more profound than others. His pain brought him to tears again. Charlie generally wore his heart on his sleeve but kept some things private, as most people do. This trip reminded him that life is short and that we must embrace the moments we have in front of us. He wiped away one last remaining tear as the train began to move.

The loudspeaker came on:

"Attention! Attention all passengers! We will arrive in Fulton, Kentucky, in about five minutes. That last stop was courtesy of a herd of cattle that wandered onto the tracks. They've moved off, and we're on our way. We're currently about eight hours behind our intended arrival time. We are sorry for the delay. For those that will be with us through to Champaign, Illinois, you are in for a treat. Anyone over 21 will be entitled to a glass of champagne, compliments of Amtrak. For all of our guests on board, your conductor will be handing out vouchers for a complimentary lunch and a drink in our dining or club car this afternoon. Again, we are sorry for the multiple delays. Hopefully, we'll be able to make it into Chicago by 8:00 pm this evening.

"NEXT STOP, FULTON, KENTUCKY!"

While this might happen on a couple of commercial airlines, Charlie thought this was a great gesture on Amtrak's part. The book *Power of Moments* by Chip and Dan Heath came to mind. They were turning what otherwise might be a sour moment for its passengers into a win.

"I guess we have to give them some grace," Charlie said, leaning toward the young lady across the aisle, trying to engage her in conversation.

"It doesn't matter much to me. I'm getting off at the next stop, and I don't know if my girlfriend will be there to pick me up. Besides, I don't get no lunch out of the deal anyway. I'm out of here." Priscilla stormed off without another word, heading for the train door. The train had not gotten up to high speed for the few minutes it took to go from the cattle to Fulton, so the slowdown and stop in Fulton didn't seem so apparent to Charlie.

As he watched a small group of people get off the train, he saw the young woman embrace her friend with a hug and lingering kiss on the lips. She was obviously glad her friend hadn't left her stranded at the station, and her attitude was 180 degrees different than when she had huffed away from Charlie. He watched the two young women walk hand in hand toward the small parking lot. *Young love,* he thought to himself.

CHAPTER 11

No Free Lunch

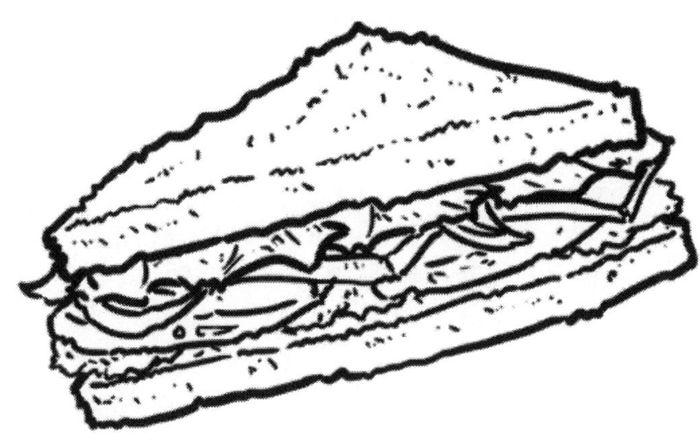

As the train pulled out of Fulton, Mack returned to his routine of checking on his passengers. This time, however, he had free lunch and drink vouchers to hand out. Eventually, he found his way to Charlie's seat.

"Here you go, Charles. One free lunch voucher and this one will get you a drink of your choice, compliments of your old friend Mack." He smiled with an ear-to-ear grin.

"Did you see that young woman with pink hair?" Charlie was not about to gossip but wondered if Mack had noticed.

"I saw her and tried speaking with her, but she dismissed me without even a smile. She got on at

Yazoo and moved from car to car, looking for a place to sit alone. I suggested that she move up here, that there were a few empty seats. When she got off the train, I handed her a voucher for lunch, which is good at any Subway restaurant; she took it from me without saying thank you, much like most people dismiss those who pass out literature on the streets." Mack appeared not to be complaining, simply telling his story. "I saw her embrace her friend. That seemed to change her tone completely."

"I agree. We talked briefly, and she seemed preoccupied and nervous about missing connections with her friend. What do you make of it, Mack?" Charlie asked as much to confirm his thoughts as he did to hear what Mack had to say.

"Remember the woman you met when you first got on the train, Essie, who worked at the New Orleans Union Station?" Charlie acknowledged him with a nod. "You didn't know her circumstances any more than you knew this young lady's situation. She may have been torn and tattered emotionally from her home life. She may be penniless and filled with mistrust for others in the world. You never know someone's situation until you walk in their shoes."

Charlie knew precisely what Mack was talking about. "You gotta give people a lot of grace these days. There are a lot of hurt people out there who have been beaten up physically, verbally, and emotionally. Lots of bullies out there, and I'm not talking about cattle."

If Charlie had learned one thing on the train, he knew Mack spoke with authority.

Mack said, "God loves all His children regardless of color, background, or lifestyle choices. That's how I see it, and I ought to know, having been working this train for so many years."

Charlie chimed in, "Mack, would you like to join me for lunch?"

"No thank you, sir. Gotta hand out some more of these vouchers and then check on our friend Mr. Quick and make sure he's okay. He might have himself a hangover after his game of cards last night."

Charlie didn't recall Jimmy talking about drinking but remembered the smell of his breath as they changed places in the sleeping car.

Mack continued, "Yes, Charles, he had a flask under his shirt tucked into his pants. He didn't want anyone to see, but I happened to notice." Mack changed the subject abruptly as if to say he didn't want to talk about Jimmy any longer. "I try to show all of our passengers the same level of service. I'll catch up with you later, Charles. More people to tend to. Enjoy your free lunch."

Charlie thought about all the business lunches he'd had over a 50-year business career. He bought more often but let others buy his lunch when appropriate. If he had three lunches out per week over fifty years, that would add up to nearly 8,000 lunch meetings. Add in dinners, breakfasts, and coffees, and that was likely over 15,000 business meals that he'd engaged in.

There were no free lunches in business because someone in the group was always looking for something. It might be a sale, a partnership, a contract extension, a job offer, or a performance review. It could have simply been the first meeting to get to know one another.

Today, though, he truly was getting a free lunch, so why not take advantage of it?

After checking his email, texting Rita, and charging his phone for a bit, Charlie headed to the dining car five cars behind his. The train flew through the southern Illinois countryside at what felt like the maximum speed the locomotive could muster. This made coordinating the railcar junctions much trickier. When he got to the last coach car before the dining car, he encountered a man who appeared to be a train stowaway standing between two of the cars at the coupling point. The man of more diminutive stature leaned against the railcar to keep his balance. With a tiny unlit cigarette butt in his hand, he had a day-old beard, wore a pair of work khaki pants, and a button-down white shirt that appeared to have been worn multiple days in a row.

"Did you hop aboard without paying a fare?" Charlie asked.

"No, sir. My kin folks paid for me to ride. Heading to Centralia, Illinois. Got some odd jobs there that will pay me something. Ain't had no work in quite a while, and I wanna work."

"When did you eat last?" Charlie asked, reaching into his pocket for the free lunch voucher.

"Last night, sir. Nice lady paid for my meal." The man stood slouched over as the train rumbled down the tracks. Charlie should have had difficulty hearing with all the noise, but he understood every word as the tight quarters had the two men close together.

"Did you get your voucher for a free lunch?"

"Yes sir, got the sandwich in my bag, figured on having it later, when I get *really* hungry. I ain't too hungry just yet." He did not look Charlie in the eye; drifters often don't because they are ashamed of the situation that got them there. Charlie realized there was no point in dragging the man through telling his story.

"Come with me. My name is Charlie and I'll help you with a good meal." Charlie opened the door and guided him through the last passenger car back toward the dining car. Some people to the left and right stared at the two of them, one freshly pressed, the other in tattered clothes and rough around the edges. Other passengers just kept to themselves, listening to whatever was in their earbuds or with their head down in a book.

When they arrived at the dining car, Charlie pulled out his voucher and approached the table where they passed out the sandwiches. He handed over his voucher and asked for his free sandwich. When the young woman handed it to him, he held onto it for himself later. "Do you have a table for one?" Charlie winked at the dining room steward without the drifter seeing him do it.

"Yes sir, we do, right over here." The steward took the two men directly to a table set up for two with nobody sitting at it yet.

"Sit right down here. Didn't get your name." Charlie took the other seat as the steward handed them each a menu. "Please ask the server to come over." He turned his head to face the man. "Bet you're hungry now, having smelled all that good food!"

"Yes, sir. Thank you. My name's Simon," he answered quietly.

The server approached their table, standing awkwardly over the two gentlemen, and asked Charlie if he would like to order.

"I'm not staying, but please provide this man with the finest meal he'd like to order. I'll take care of the bill." Simon started to protest, but Charlie said, "Don't you worry, Simon." Charlie pulled out two crisp $100 bills. "Young lady, here is $100 for his food. When the bill is paid, give yourself a $20 tip and give this gentleman the remainder of the change. Simon, this is for you," Charlie handed him another $100 bill. "Safe travels, sir. Our paths may cross on the train later, but if they don't, best wishes to you with that work you've got lined up."

Simon was speechless but eventually said, "God bless you, and thanks ever so much."

"CARBONDALE! CARBONDALE, ILLINOIS NEXT!
NEXT STOP, CARBONDALE, ILLINOIS!"

Charlie couldn't know whether Simon's story of work in Centralia was true. It didn't much matter to him as he felt compelled to help the man, regardless. Charlie recalled so many other times in his life when he'd done similar things for people who had life challenges and were down on their luck. He contrasted those situations with panhandlers who worked the busiest traffic corners in Cincinnati or Chicago. Some had cell phones, packs of cigarettes, and sometimes what looked like a well-fed dog, helping them look for sympathy. Charlie had once seen what he thought was a homeless couple pick up their things and get into a late-model Cadillac parked just around the corner from where they were working. While he wasn't skeptical of everyone, he would often help those who least expected it.

Upon returning to his seat after the short stop in Carbondale, Charlie ate his free sandwich. Since it wasn't school time, he noticed that there wasn't a rush for seats by students attending Southern Illinois University. He pulled out his copy of his friend Gary Moore's book, *Playing with the Enemy.* He had brought it along knowing he'd be in New Orleans, where Gary had written the book before and after the Katrina hurricane devastated the city.

Gary had inspired Charlie for two main reasons. *Playing with the Enemy* was Gary's first of several books and had launched his role as a successful author. Secondly, Gary was among the most positive people that Charlie knew. At every opportunity, he encouraged Charlie to write more, even when Charlie didn't feel motivated to.

Mack had a knack for just showing up when Charlie least expected it. "Something on your mind, Charles?" Mack could see that Charlie had a book in his lap.

"Just thinking about my old friend Gary who used to encourage my writing. He died of stomach cancer, that was a few years ago now. Gary authored this book about his dad's experience with baseball and World War II. I first met Gary at the Museum of Science and Industry in Chicago at one of his book signings. I identified with his dad, Gene, who was the main character in his book. Gene was a baseball catcher here in Southern Illinois. He played for the Egyptians in Sesser when he was far younger than most who were playing. Gary was known as America's storyteller and told a good story with this book."

"Sounds like you've respected your friend a great deal. Why do you carry the book around with you?"

"I guess I find things like this inspirational, I've collected all sorts of trinkets over the years. Books can be therapeutic. Certainly, the Bible can be." Charlie knew that Mack was a religious man, as he had spoken respectfully about spiritual things more than once. "I have access to the online version of the Bible on my phone everywhere I go," Mack didn't seem surprised. "But there is something about the turning of pages of a book and the smell of paper that makes it different."

Mack listened more intently to Charlie's story.

Charlie continued. "I read the Bible for the first time in a hotel room; it was a Gideon in the desk drawer. I was on a business trip that was not going well for me. I had been traveling quite a bit and missed being at home. I didn't go to church at that point, yet I felt a calling to read from the book of James. It was eye-opening."

"Struggling, were you?" Mack asked.

"Yes, in several ways that are hard to describe. That was so long ago. What came of it allowed me to study more, read more, and learn more than I ever could have imagined. I also met several other business professionals who showed me the Way. I've looked back at my life and recognized that God was beside me many times, which I didn't realize at the time. When I gave financially, it felt good, but I also seemed to make more sales or was blessed with a new business relationship. When I gave my time to volunteer efforts, I learned more about life and felt better about myself. My life felt enriched when I shared my expertise with a young student as a tutor or mentored a young professional." Charlie paused.

"You mean that you gave of your time, talent, and treasure?" Mack asked.

"Yes, I have tried to do so anyway. At times, we struggled financially, and yet I looked around at so many who were homeless without knowing where their next meal was coming from. Most of us in the United States have more in our abundance, and yet often we squander it."

Charlie continued to talk in a continuous ramble that satisfied him and him alone. "You know what I mean?"

Charlie looked over his shoulder and throughout the passenger car, but Mack was nowhere to be found.

"CENTRALIA! CENTRALIA, ILLINOIS, NEXT!
NEXT STOP, CENTRALIA, ILLINOIS!"

Charlie realized that he knew a little about many things and not much about any one subject. However, there were also some topics that he could talk about all day. Indeed, everyone who knew him knew that if they chose to speak with Charlie about baseball or business topics, he could go down a very long rabbit trail. As the train slowed to a stop, Charlie looked out the window hoping to see Simon one last time, but he didn't. With his weary travel, Charlie longed for that comfortable bed.

Since Rita hadn't picked up his call, Charlie texted her to tell her about his fantastic adventures.

Chapter 12

Reflections

Hey Babe. Working or up to talking? The train has just left Centralia, and Effingham is the next stop. NEXT STOP EFFINGHAM, ILLINOIS. I have had some incredible experiences, and as often happens when I'm on the road, I've met some fascinating people. If you aren't working or out in the yard, call me. I won't have dinner on the train; I decided to hold out for ribs at Miller's Pub on Wabash. Something tells me we may get in later than the conductor thinks. Please remind me to tell you about

Mack and the year 1914. Love you the most. *smooch emoji*

Charlie decided to switch seats, moving his things across the aisle so that he was on the east side of the northbound train so that the sun wasn't shining in his face. The rest of the trip into Chicago would be filled with more places he'd seen or experienced over his lifetime. He had traveled the state of Illinois extensively, and there was not a corner of the state he hadn't at least gone through on his business and personal travels.

The name Effingham created vivid thoughts that ran through Charlie's mind. A company in Effingham had purchased one of the first companies that he had worked for. Each time he saw the company name on the headquarters building, it reminded him of those times. He had also interviewed for a position in Effingham many years ago. While he didn't get the position, Charlie remembered how kind the people at the company were.

Years later, Charlie would be back in Effingham, dating Rita and visiting all the local establishments to listen to live music with her. That seemed like a lifetime ago, and yet it wasn't.

Mack came back through the aisle and noticed that Charlie had moved seats. "Charles, what's up with the change in seats?"

Charlie avoided the question for the time being, "Hey Mack, I was talking with you a while ago, and when I looked up you were gone. Where'd you run off to?"

"I had to tend to another passenger in need, Jimmy Quick. He had to be removed from the train at the last stop. He was having difficulty breathing. Thankfully, one of the other conductors was able to radio ahead and have an ambulance waiting when the train stopped." Mack was leaving out details in an effort to be both brief and respectful at the same time.

"I didn't see or hear anything. Was the ambulance in stealth mode? Were the paramedics able to help him?" Charlie was, of course, concerned for the man he'd met the night before.

"None of us wanted to draw attention to the incident, and yes, Jimmy appeared to be okay, but to be safe, they took him to a nearby hospital. We tried to take care of him with little commotion." Mack was the consummate professional.

Returning to the topic of their earlier conversation, Mack said, "As you know, I was hearing every word you shared. As I left, you stopped talking aloud."

Charlie balked. "Is that possible? I really thought I was talking with you!"

"That happens to me all the time." Mack smiled playfully.

He then changed the subject. "Interested in doubling that bet we wagered earlier?"

"About what time we'll get into Union Station?" Charlie remembered Mack's 8:35 pm prediction.

"No, I was talking about the Cubs and Sox. I heard both lost their afternoon games. The Cubs lost at Wrigley to the Giants 6-0, and the White Sox lost in New York 5-4 against the Yankees. Greg Allen hit a two-run homer in the bottom of the 9th to win it. Tough season again for both of them, Charles. How will we settle that bet about one of them winning the

World Series this year?" Mack appeared to be serious about the bet.

"Who hit a home run, Greg Allen?" Charlie smiled. "I never agreed to that bet. I shook hands with you on the time in the station bet, but nothing about the World Series, that's for sure!" Charlie's animation was almost laughable. "There is no way I would bet on the Cubs or Sox this year. Besides, I now live in Cincinnati. Do you know how the Reds did?"

"Off day for travel, play tomorrow in Pittsburg before coming home to Cincinnati for a Fourth of July series against the Cardinals." Mack sounded like a sports broadcaster with his knowledgeable response.

"What? No statistical analysis of their box score or pitching staff?" Charlie teased.

The two laughed as their conversation about baseball went on and on.

"EFFINGHAM! EFFINGHAM, ILLINOIS, NEXT.
NEXT STOP, EFFINGHAM, ILLINOIS."

"Mack, you know what?" Charlie started down a completely different path. "I met my wife Rita through an online dating app. She lived not far from here, in fact, just over those fields." Charlie pointed out the window. "We've been together for so long; sometimes, my life with my former wife seems like a lifetime ago. Do you think that's normal?"

"As you know, Charles, 'Normal' is the sister city to Bloomington, Illinois, just off Interstate 74 and Interstate 55. Old Route 66 runs through there, as does the train between St. Louis and Chicago." Mack was being playful again.

"Thanks for the geography lesson. Nobody knows those roads better than me." Charlie had lived in Normal for many years. "Do you think people find ways of living in the moment without concern for the past?"

For the first time Charlie could recall, Mack rubbed his chin and appeared perplexed, not having an immediate response. "I guess that depends on many factors, Charles. What helps you reconcile your past?"

The question got turned around on Charlie, and he spoke to Mack directly. "We each have our own set of circumstances that we have to live with, our crosses to bear, so to speak. We each do the best we can when we can. If we live in the moment, knowing that we can't change the past and that tomorrow will be there when it comes, then we can live in the moment. Rita and I try to do that every day. She never says NO to my crazy ideas and often goes along for the ride because it is far more fun than sitting around waiting for things to happen."

Mack quietly recited the Serenity Prayer to Charlie. "Remember this prayer: God, Grant me the serenity to accept the things that I cannot change. The courage to change the things that I can. And the wisdom to know the difference."

Charlie smiled. "Mack, I have leaned into that prayer more times than I can count, personally and professionally. I have seen some major challenges in my business life and sometimes just wanted to *fix* them. Other times I just needed to sit on a box and let the problems play themselves out."

Charlie continued. "As I said earlier, as I was getting back on the train in Jackson, there are three kinds of people. Those who make things happen, those who watch things happen, and those who *wonder* what happened.

"What does that mean to you?" Mack encouraged.

"I guess there are times when I watch things happen in business. We have to let younger people make their mistakes and learn from them. Didn't always think about it that way. I wanted to catch them doing things right and often helped them more than I should have. I have a much greater trust level today with younger people than I used to. We have some amazing young people in business today, but we have to have a level of trust."

Mack noticed the train coming to a stop. "Gotta run, Charles. We need to help passengers get on and off here in...where are we? Oh yes, Effingham." He scooted down the aisle toward the doorway.

Charlie traveled so often back in the day that he sometimes forgot which city or hotel he was at. He'd heard the same things from other salespeople and traveling executives, some of whom always frequented one hotel chain or another to get the perks and points. The same held true for airlines and point systems; Charlie had his share of free nights and free flights. He glanced out the window and felt the familiarity of Effingham fill his soul. Illinois would always be his home, and because of Rita's connection to Effingham, it was another home away from home.

Knowing this part of the route meant that Mattoon would be next in about 30 minutes, Champaign would follow, and then Kankakee after that. From there, getting into the city of Chicago was a breeze because seeing familiar buildings and landmarks would pass the time quickly. Charlie's suburban Chicago trips from all points North, West, and South had a similar feel about them, just different towns, station names, and distances to walk to a bus or the L train.

Charlie felt at home already but was still at least three hours away from Chicago's Union Station. He checked his phone: No text message from Rita. Charlie took a selfie for the first time in 24 hours and sent it to Rita with the Effingham sign whizzing by in the background. It was hard to read, but she'll get the point:

Just left Effingham. This pic is the first one I've taken this entire trip. Wow!

CHAPTER 13

Champaign Celebration

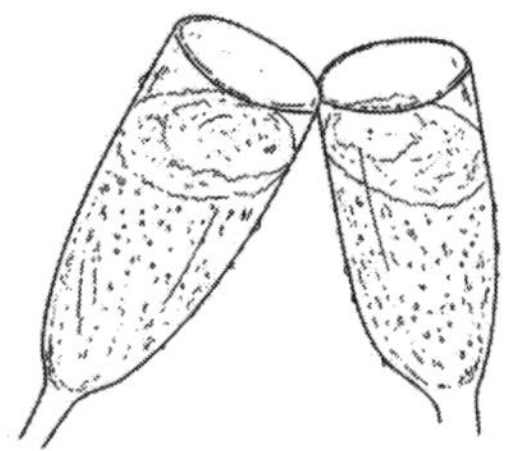

Charlie recalled traveling into Chicago from various directions using the local rail lines over the years. Each line had a different feel to it because of the towns and neighborhoods it passed through. He remembered coming in from the south following the 2016 Cubs World Series Championship when he celebrated in Grant Park with two million other crazy fans. It was a warm November day, and Charlie remembered thinking about global warming as he flew his large royal blue "W" flag. Baseball isn't meant to be played in November, and the 2016 series would bring the first-ever Game 7 after Halloween.

As the train passed the historic station in Mattoon, Charlie marveled at the size of the building. As another flag-stop on the route, the train slowed down as it passed. Without anyone scheduled to get off the train or needing to board, the locomotive began speeding up as it passed through the town. Charlie decided to take this opportunity to freshen up and use the restroom.

Looking in the mirror of the tiny restroom, Charlie noticed his day-old beard creating a rough look about him. Otherwise, clean-shaven, he splashed some water on his face and felt more refreshed. He had done so over the years on many plane trips, simply to get up, stretch his legs, and pass the time quicker in the air. Without much room to hang out, the train restroom served its purpose without additional luxury.

Walking back to his seat, Charlie noticed that the train car had a little more excitement to it. People seemed to be talking with one another, which was different than had been the case for most of the trip.

"CHAMPAIGN! CHAMPAIGN, ILLINOIS, NEXT!
NEXT STOP, CHAMPAIGN, ILLINOIS!"

The club car staff had come through the train earlier with plastic champagne flutes, the announcer came on the loudspeaker once more. "As we approach Champaign, Illinois, your passenger car conductor will bring the champagne around, and you'll hear a countdown on our speaker system." Some passengers heard the instructions; others had to be told by their seat neighbors. Charlie was always prepared for a celebration of any size, shape, or color.

In various companies Charlie worked at or managed, a celebratory bell hung in the lobby, front office, or otherwise prominent place. One company where Charlie was on the leadership team expected its employees to drop what they were doing for 2-3 minutes when they heard the loud ringing of the bell. The team would get to learn about what sales had been made, and the salesperson of record would share some of the details for the team to understand. Most importantly, the salesperson would thank the other team members who helped make it happen. Sometimes, a sales engineer did a product demonstration that made the difference; other times, it was a receptionist who made the client feel welcome during their company visit.

"Nothing starts until the sale is made." Charlie considered it among his first lessons in business.

He thought about another that was top of mind. *"All things are possible with MARGIN."* So many small to mid-sized companies had pricing or sales models that left them unprofitable and needing help to grow or pay their staff appropriately. Charlie had found through his recent consulting engagements that some companies still had to be reminded that they needed to make a profit in order to grow.

Soon, Charlie heard a cork-pop, an easily recognized, universal sound. Mack was walking down the aisle with a bottle of champagne and had a smile on his face. "Here you are, my friend. Charles, please hold your glass steady while I pour." Mack filled Charlie's flute.

"Would you like some help with the other passengers?" Charlie offered.

"If you would like to pop the next bottle, that would be helpful." Mack was responsible for the front two cars and only a few passengers that still needed to be filled up. Charlie was happy to help. "Many hands..." Mack started.

"Make light work!" Charlie chimed in. He recalled countless church and chamber of commerce events where he was thankful for the help in cleaning up the venue. *"Those who stick around to help clean up get that extra satisfaction that others don't."* Charlie realized there were so many lessons that had been ingrained in him over the years. Another he recalled: *"A job completed is ten times more satisfying than a job started and unfinished."*

The intercom squealed, and a voice came across loud and clear: "All guests bound for Chicago, this is your onboard lead engineer speaking. While I didn't start with you in Louisiana, I am bringing this big locomotive and all of you into the great city of Chicago. On behalf of Amtrak and our entire crew of service staff and chefs, porters in the sleeping berths, conductors, and our engineering crew, we would like to thank you for your patience with the sometimes-unpredictable process of train travel. We recognize that you have a choice, and the easy one is certainly to fly when you have a distance to travel. We believe that in traveling by train, you are receiving value for the fare that you pay and that we can provide an experience rather than just a mode of transportation."

Charlie was beginning to wonder how long this toast would go on, even though he admittedly was known for exceeding his time limit when given a microphone or up on stage.

The announcement continued: "We thank you for traveling with us, and while we know that we are not quite at our final destination, our team felt that Champaign, Illinois, would be a suitable place to have this toast. So, here's to our guests! On the count of three...One...Two...Three!"

Everyone raised their champagne flutes and took a sip. Some completed the toast with one large swig. Everyone cheered.

Charlie was reminded of his time with the chamber of commerce, whose core focus was supporting, connecting, and celebrating business success. Charlie's ability to build corporate culture had expanded to helping create a sense of community. Everyone seemed to buy into the concept of the Flywheel, which Charlie taught about regularly. The flywheel business model was based on his obsession with delighting chamber members and his desire to be responsive. So many companies had become complacent and waiting for the business to come to them. Instead, Charlie taught others to have responsive staff that did a better job of engaging their clients. He helped many to see that this level of service created a community of raving fans.

"May I take your flute and any other trash?" The service staff member held open a large, heavy plastic bag in front of Charlie.

"Here you go," Charlie dropped in some papers and his champagne flute. Charlie had countless trinkets around his office that represented a trip, conference, or sales event; however, this was not a souvenir moment. Charlie even had a small brass dinner bell that Rita had given him to ring when a celebration moment came, even if he was alone and in his office. *A win is still a win*, she always told him.

Charlie looked around the passenger car and was aware that people were still engaged and talking to one another over the backs of their chairs and actually having conversations. One woman was showing off pictures of her family, while a young man showed another guy a funny video he'd created with his family German shepherd.

What was the difference, and why at this point? Charlie wondered. At that moment, he knew exactly what to do, but first, he had to think through his plan. Once he narrowed down his thoughts into one question, Charlie began wandering the train car, listening in on individual conversations.

He began asking, "What changed the direction of this train trip and allowed you the comfort to connect with fellow passengers at this particular moment in time?" After discussing this with two small groups, Charlie knew he did not need a piece of paper or a Survey Monkey website to get to the bottom of his query.

The first two people he asked responded, "We were just wondering about that same thing. We knew that it was not the alcohol, that little taste of champagne wouldn't do it, but we decided two things happened." Charlie was attentive and in full listening mode. "First of all, we had the anticipation of the event coming. We'd been told earlier in the day that we should expect this surprise in Champaign, Illinois. Then the train leadership delivered. We just weren't satisfied; we were blown away!"

"What is the second reason?" Charlie asked.

"The engineer came over the loudspeaker and said, 'Thank you!'. We felt appreciated. Companies today need to do a better job of making their customers feel good. Carol, that is your name, right? Carol said she'll be back on the train again, and I said that Carol should write an amazing review about her experience and their team. Encourage others to try the train instead of flying."

Charlie thanked them for sharing. "I don't want to interrupt your conversation and getting acquainted. Enjoy the rest of your trip. My name is Charlie."

"We know who you are," Carol said. "We've heard you and Mack talking throughout the trip. We were just saying that we can tell you carry a level of confidence that most people don't these days."

"Thank you so much for the compliment." While Charlie didn't blush, he was not always comfortable accepting praise.

He moved on to the second set of passengers, two men in their twenties. When asking the same question, Charlie got a completely different answer that excited him just as much.

"We went on Facebook Live during the toast, and it blew up with viewers!" The first young man shared his experience. "We just started showing the people on board having fun. People don't have as much fun in groups like this as they used to. We were just discussing that everyone we know wants a fun experience. They are tired of the mundane. We just showed off our experience in recorded form. We're going to put a short Reel together before we get to the city, should be posted soon." The young man asked Charlie, "Is that what you thought our answer would be?"

Charlie answered quickly, "Guys, I'm old. I know that these things you're talking about make an impact, but at my age, I'm just hoping that your generation can articulate the message in a caring way that personalizes it. GREAT WORK! Thanks for sharing."

Just then, Mack came up behind Charlie with another man. "Charlie, this is Engineer Stevenson. He would like to thank you personally for making the trip enjoyable for multiple passengers." Mack encouraged them to shake hands. He took a picture of the two of them with Charlie's cell phone, and the two men chatted briefly.

"Charlie, thanks again for choosing to ride the train when you had the option to fly. We hope that you give us a try another time, and please encourage others to do so. I need to talk with other passengers, but it was nice to meet you." Stevenson patiently walked around the passenger car, thanking anyone willing to talk with him. He looked like an ocean cruise captain in his formal apparel and knew his locomotive and its passengers. When done in Charlie's car, Stevenson moved toward the back of the train, presumably doing the same thing repeatedly.

Charlie remembered a 25th-anniversary celebration at a Champaign company he'd managed. He thought about the various companies that he led. The changes took a toll on him in multiple ways personally, but Charlie learned a great deal along the way. He was most proud of all the quality people he worked with across Central Illinois, attended church with, and met personally. While his professional accomplishments were many, he was most proud of his relationships over 15 years in that community.

"KANKAKEE! KANKAKEE, ILLINOIS, NEXT!
NEXT STOP, KANKAKEE, ILLINOIS!"

CHAPTER 14

Chicago Roots

Charlie attended Illinois Wesleyan University in the hopes of playing baseball and getting a quality education at the same time. Various circumstances forced a choice between baseball and a degree. Charlie hadn't been an outstanding student; some subjects came far too easy, making him bored and uninterested. As he progressed in school, the coursework became far more challenging for him.

Charlie didn't pledge a fraternity but was able to be a social connector on campus and built friendships with many diverse groups. He was a night owl back then, staying up until all hours playing Euchre and hanging out with friends, but certainly not studying. An occasional all-nighter was necessary because of deadlines and procrastination. Charlie had started his career in sales right after college.

Charlie was a procrastinator until he found a business mentor who taught him many of the time-management techniques, which he subsequently passed on to others. Do, Delay, Delegate, and Drop were 4-D stories of the past that came rushing through Charlie's head.

What's most important and urgent? These are things to focus on. *Do* them and do them well. *Delay* those tasks that aren't urgent but need to be done by you, and you alone. *Delegate* those tasks that either someone else is better at or stretch someone else's abilities; otherwise, simply take it off your plate. *Drop* those things that really don't need to be done. Charlie had been following this format for years to increase his productivity, and he instilled these simple rules in the teams he managed. Charlie had shared Brian Tracy's book, Eat That Frog at least a million times — well, maybe a hundred. The book focuses on doing the most challenging tasks first so that you have a high degree of satisfaction and productivity for the remainder of the day.

"Charles, are you talking to yourself again?" Mack had developed a specific cadence that allowed him to appear to be everywhere but also be present when the time was right. Back in the day, many would have called this practice 'Walk around management.' Mack had his walking down to a science. "Talking to yourself can be a good habit, best performed alone unless you want someone to look at you strangely. Charles, didn't you say you are originally from Chicago?"

"Yes sir, born and raised." Charlie had to clarify his response. "I was actually born in the City of Chicago, but our family lived in the near west suburbs of Cicero, Berwyn, and LaGrange. When someone from Cincinnati asks where you went to school, they mean high school. When someone in Chicago asks where you grew up, it means which neighborhood or suburb. I simply tell people I'm from Chicago unless they want to drill into which part of the Chicagoland area."

That made sense to Mack, who was interested in his passenger's history. "Go on," he encouraged.

"My parents were married very young and divorced by the time I was seven. I had some challenging times but got through them, as most kids do. My parents were each married four times. That information shocks most people when I tell them." Charlie watched for Mack's reaction.

"Doesn't surprise me. Not much I haven't heard before, especially with the number of passengers sharing their stories with me."

"I have told people over the years," Charlie continued, "that if you take all the awful things that happened in your life, all that stuff that eats at you and your inner self, and you put it in the middle of a circle, you can see it clearly in front of you. Then, picture everyone else you know doing the same thing and sitting around the outside of the same circle, looking at their own garbage in the middle. If you were then asked to walk into the circle and take back some of the garbage, each person would likely take their own because they knew what it was. They knew how much it stunk, but they knew how to deal with it. That might not be the case with someone else's challenges or junk. Does that make sense, Mack?"

Mack rubbed his chin like a wise professor might. "Charles, that is one deep thought with many dimensions. I'll have to get back to you on that one, but you keep it close at hand. I'll bet it has served you well all these years." Mack could tell that Charlie was pleased by his response.

Charlie continued. "I was very impulsive when I was younger. I jumped in, feet first, so to speak, without considering how deep the pool was. Thankfully, when I felt like I was drowning in a personal or business dilemma, the right book, person, or idea came to me with a potential solution. I say potential only because I think people today, and maybe in the past, don't consider options."

"A wise observation indeed, Charles."

"In my business career, if I chose the first and only option, I would have been dead in the water nine times out of ten. It was asking for advice, gathering consensus when necessary, researching a topic, and asking my peers in other places that got me out of many a jam. When I asked others for their input, it also lifted them up and made them feel involved in the decision, even if the ultimate decision wasn't theirs to make."

“Charles, we are approaching our last stop,” Mack said and was just then interrupted by the loudspeaker:

“HOMEWOOD! HOMEWOOD, ILLINOIS, NEXT.
LAST STOP BEFORE CHICAGO UNION STATION.
NEXT STOP, HOMEWOOD, ILLINOIS.”

“I have to make final preparations for our arrival into Chicago and will be passing through the cars more frequently over the final portion of the trip. If you need anything, anything at all, just flag me down.” Mack looked down at his pocket watch. "Right on time Charlie, looks like 8:35 pm on the dot.”

“How do you know that? We could stop again, or something else could delay us between here and Chicago. Why are you so certain?” Charlie tried to find a wrinkle in Mack's otherwise cleanly pressed conductor's uniform.

“Charles, I've been on this trip countless times and take into consideration all the possibilities. When you were a traveling salesperson in Chicago, you drove everywhere, right? You didn't have a GPS or smartphone to guide you back then. You used your instincts about leaving early and considered traffic patterns and the time of day. You probably listened to traffic reports to know whether the Kennedy, Edens, or Eisenhower Expressway would be the best route. You planned for the unexpected so that you would be early — Lombardi time, right?”

Charlie admitted that he tried to accomplish too many things, see too many people, and ran behind far too often back then. "I tried to be on time, but sometimes it just didn't work out that way. Good intentions —I always had good intentions to be on time. Today, I am much better, and maybe it has to do with my age or a better calendaring system, but GPS and traffic slowdowns that show up on my phone sure help. Haven't been late to an appointment in a long time."

"I will leave you with this, Charles." Charlie listened closely as Mack spoke. "Don't beat yourself up over things that have happened in the past. Focus on the here and now. The future will take care of itself, and you will be just fine." Mack was profoundly serious; he winked his right eye. "You want to return my coin to me now, or wait until we get into Union Station at exactly 8:35 pm?"

"I'll hold onto it for a while longer, Mack. The trip isn't quite over yet." Charlie smiled back at his friend.

The stop at Homewood was brief, and the train moved on, but at a much slower pace as it moved northward, ever closer to the city. The enthusiastic conversations that had been taking place at and after the Champaign stop seem to have quieted. Another evening was ending, and having passed the longest day of the year, the sun lingered in the sky to the west of the Windy City.

Charlie thought to himself that he had much to look forward to for the rest of the week in Chicago, especially lunch with his baseball teammates on Friday.

He thought about his childhood trips home from Wrigley Field on afternoons like this. There weren't any night games until 1989, so daytime in the summer was baseball on the Northside. His mom would give him enough money for a bleacher seat, lunch, and transportation to and from the game. Charlie and his friends were just 12 or 13 and without cell phones to track their whereabouts — they got home when they got home. Charlie would have to remember to ask his buddies on Friday what they remembered about those days so that they could have a lengthy conversation about it. For now, Charlie sat close to the window and marveled at the city towers in the distance and the setting sun shimmering off their westerly windows.

Chapter 15

Coming in Hot

Charlie texted his manager friend at the Hyatt Regency to alert him of his timing. He'd arrive later at the hotel due to his need for that full rack of ribs at Miller's Pub. His phone was unusually quiet from Rita, but again there was nothing he could do but wait to hear from her. She could be tied up volunteering somewhere, planting in the pollinator garden, or be without power. Charlie wasn't one to worry.

The two men who had done the live video came up to Charlie for advice. “Sir, we’ve heard you sharing business principles during the train ride, and we have a question for you. We've been talking since Champaign and think we might want to start a business together, maybe a marketing or video production company. After all, we're both working for companies with jobs that aren't very satisfying.”

Charlie pulled out two business cards and handed them to the young men, "This may seem like an odd answer coming from someone as old as me, but here goes.” Charlie cleared his throat as if he were to start a long speech. “ARE YOU CRAZY?!!!” He gave the two of them a look like he was a madman. It appeared out of character to them, but of course, they weren’t familiar with Charlie's sense of humor.

The two men stepped back with startled looks on their faces. Charlie continued, “Did I scare you?”

“You sure did,” both agreed.

“Well, the fact is, you should be. Starting a business is not for the faint of heart. It has to be wisely organized with a business plan, a financial plan, and a marketing plan. Have either of you thought about these things?”

“We haven't,” the first man said. “The two of us just met, and we have only talked for the last hour or two. We thought we'd ask for your advice.”

“I’m sorry, I’m afraid we’re off on the wrong foot. What are your names?”

"I'm Ramahal, and he's Karl.” They seemed like levelheaded young men.

“What I'm trying to help you see is that it takes a great deal of planning to build and run a successful business. Businesses today, especially those formed from great ideas and in partnerships like the two of you, fail due to lack of funding." Charlie spoke as a man of authority now.

Charlie continued, "My advice is to really get to know one another. Spend some time together after work, grab a beer somewhere, or meet in one of your homes where you can talk for hours. If you need a good place, I can recommend Miller's at Wabash and Adams under the L tracks." Charlie chuckled because he knew the staff there would let men like Karl and Ramahal stay all day if they liked, as it was good for business.

"Brainstorm ideas between the two of you before you do anything else and take lots of notes. You'll see where your respective passions are and if one of you is naturally a visionary and another an integrator." Charlie knew that these terms were foreign to them. "Which of you had the idea to begin with?"

"Karl did," Ramahal said. "I like to see things through and execute plans."

"Sounds like a match made in EOS," Charlie said and smiled at the two young men.

"Where is Eos?" asked one of the guys. It sounded like a foreign country or a distant planet to them. But they were genuinely curious, which Charlie enjoyed.

"E.O.S. stands for Entrepreneurial Operating System." I can introduce you to someone who can share more, or you can pick up the book *Traction* by Gino Wickman. Are you familiar with SCORE?"

"You aren't talking about a sports score, are you Charlie?" They figured it was another acronym.

"SCORE is a group of experienced coaches that volunteer, people like me. They help young business owners like you get started on the right track. You can see many tracks here in the freight yard, right?" Charlie pointed out the window, and the men nodded. "Each of those tracks leads somewhere. Hopefully, ours will land us inside the Union Station where we want to be, as it's our destination."

The passenger rail system shared space with the freight trains throughout Chicago, and they had the right of way in most instances. The stops and starts of the train were very noticeable by this time.

"You want to have people and resources at your disposal when you're just getting started. Have you heard of an incubator? I don't mean the kind you use for hatching chicks either." Both men shook their heads. "Here in Chicago, plenty of incubators are willing to help you with business plans and mentor you in the important lessons of starting a business. Angel funding companies are around to help with financial start-ups, but you have to have a foundational start. Don't go quitting your day jobs just yet. If it is meant to be, it will be."

Karl and Ramahal realized that Charlie's outburst at the beginning of the conversation was a visual reminder to be cautious about starting a partnership. Still, they were glad that they had continued the conversation. "Do you have a LinkedIn profile, Charlie? Karl and I will hit you up...I mean, send you a connection request," Ramahal said.

"SIR...A connection request, Sir!" Charlie had that sarcastic tone, and the three of them laughed, then exchanged information."

The two men moved to their seats and began discussing what Charlie had said. He knew that this may or may not bear fruit, but without fertilizing the entrepreneurial spirit in young people, the world would not have the innovation it has today.

Charlie noticed that the air conditioning, which had been significantly cooler than the outdoors, was now virtually non-existent. Charlie felt similar to how he did at the beginning of the trip in New Orleans; the humidity of Chicago in late June had caught up with the cooling systems, and Charlie was getting uncomfortable.

Other passengers were beginning to shed any layers of clothes that they could. Newspapers and magazines were being used as makeshift fans to at least move the air around their faces.

Charlie thought, "This is uncomfortable but not unbearable." He'd been to Alcatraz Prison in San Francisco Bay during a mid-summer day when the humidity and temperature were in the mid-90s. Charlie had been in 117-degree heat at Hoover Dam in June, and although it was a dry heat, ice cream still melted faster than he could eat it, he remembered. Charlie didn't want to think about the heat; it only made it worse.

By contrast, Soldiers Field at the 1985 Bears playoff game during their Superbowl run was the coldest Charlie had ever been. Feet so cold that it took two days for them to thaw. Thinking about the cold didn't help him either.

Charlie looked at Ramahal and Karl. They seemed unaffected by the rising temperatures. However, everyone else in the train car was complaining profusely. You could hear the nasty tone in the passengers' voices. Charlie overheard one woman say that she was never going to ride the train again and was going to write a scathing online review. Charlie was starting to get mad, and it usually took a great deal for his blood to boil. Acting quickly, he decided to make a difference and stood up to make an announcement.

"May I have your attention!" Some people stopped chatting, but others still talked loudly. "Excuse me, can I have your attention!" Charlie motioned to Ramahal and Karl to see which might know how to whistle. He put two fingers in his mouth and gave the universal blow sign. Karl picked up on it and gave the loudest whistle he could. That got everyone's attention, and Charlie took to his soapbox.

"Now that I have your attention, my name is Charlie, and I've been on this train since New Orleans. How many of you, by show of hands, have as well?" Four hands went up. "How many since Jackson?" A few more hands went up.

"Let's suffice it to say that we've all had a long journey, isn't that right?" Everyone agreed. "When the train was delayed earlier, the company gave free lunches away, right? Free drinks, too. They tried to make it right despite having freight train delays and cows on the tracks."

Charlie noticed Mack in the back of the car being silent and hidden behind the passengers, who were now intently focused on Charlie's speech. "Most of you have been on since Champaign and had a toast provided by your carrier, am I right?" Everyone nodded.

“These two young men right here have formed a new friendship and may even start a company together because they met on this train today. That's pretty cool in my book. Well, I didn't mean to use a temperature pun...get it? Cool?” The train car groaned in unison. Charlie laughed. “You get my point. Some of you may have made new friends, and in the process, that person may change your life. Okay, that's kind of what?” Charlie encouraged the passengers to say, “COOL!”. "Now come on, you can do better than that? That's kind of COOL!” The car was cheering.

“I want to ask all of you a serious question. Do you think a train engineer who has come through and shaken all of your hands, thanked you for hanging with them, and provided you with champagne INTENTIONALLY turned off the air conditioning just so that you could arrive at Union Station a hot mess? I don't believe it for a second, not a New York second or even a Chicago second.” A couple more groans came, but people were getting his point.

He continued, "I ask you this: You have all been to a Fourth of July celebration, right? Picnics, parades, festivals where it was so hot that a second lemon shakeup didn't even satisfy your thirst. Come on, you all know what I'm talking about. Did you gripe and complain about the heat? Of course, you didn't because you couldn't do anything about it any more than you can at this very moment. Now, I'm going to get serious for just a minute. Show of hands, how many of you are service veterans or have a son or daughter in or have been in the service? How many of you have parents or grandparents that fought in a war sometime somewhere?" Almost every hand was raised and proudly raised high.

"Do you think that they bemoaned being in a foxhole or running up a training hill at Camp wherever in sweltering heat? I am sure they did, but they endured. Folks, this is a first-world problem if you think about it. Many places on this earth don't have electricity, let alone know what air conditioning is. They rely on the shade of a tree and a wistful breeze to keep them from burning under a blistering sun." Charlie caught a smile on Mack's face in the back of the room. He knew precisely where Charlie was going with the completion of his speech.

"Each of us is so privileged to be free in this country of ours. We can eat what we want, say what we want, and do whatever we want whenever we want to do it. We do so because our founding fathers fought hard for us; and here we will celebrate our Independence Day next week. I will bet all of you that you'll be celebrating in the heat hotter than we have to endure for the remainder of this trip. Who knows what time it is?"

"8:30!" shouted the woman who had been complaining the loudest.

"Mack is in the back. He picked up our slack and provided us with a snack. No wisecracks from the back!" The passenger car laughed heartily as young Ramahal and Karl led them in a cheer. "Mack, how long until we are in the station?"

"We are actually in the station already, but we'll come to a complete stop in just four, no, *three* minutes." Mack looked at his pocket watch; it would be precisely 8:35 pm when they got to the platform.

He continued, "On behalf of our entire staff, we hope you enjoyed your journey with us. If you can forgive a brief malfunction of our cooling unit, we hope you return and ride our system of trains again. Please be sure to take all of your belongings with you. Our cleaning crew will be through the compartments so any help you can have with trash will be greatly appreciated. Please watch your step. Welcome to Union Station, Chicago, Illinois. If you would, please give our friend Charlie a round of applause for entertaining and reminding us about what is important when you're hot under the collar." The train car cheered and gave Charlie continual high-fives as they lined up to leave the train. A couple of people went out of their way to say thank you and offer a prayer of safe passage for the remainder of Charlie's trip.

Chapter 16

Settling a Bet

The passengers departed quickly; after all, they had places to go and people to see. Secondarily, the heated train had caused them to be uncomfortable, and they needed to move. If the last few miles into the station had turned into hours, Charlie and Mack would have had a mutiny on their hands.

Mack didn't have any doorway responsibilities, and he had said goodbye to the other special passengers he'd met on this particular trip. He reserved his final conversation for Charlie and a compliment for thinking on his feet. "Charlie, that may have been the best tap dance I've ever seen without a pair of tap-dancing shoes. Where did that idea come from?" Mack was serious; he marveled at Charlie's ingenuity.

"Mack, when you've been around the business world for as long as I have, you often have to fake it until you make it. I just looked at the situation, knowing that we needed to pivot the minds of the people who were hot and bothered. What better way to do that than to be brutally honest and speak from the heart? I didn't know exactly what I would say, it was instinctive. That rhyme, well, I may have pulled it out of thin air. Sometimes, you have to challenge the paradigm."

Charlie continued. "Mack, I talk with business owners all the time about the importance of working *on* their business 20% of the time and *in* their business 80% of the time. You appear to be the kind of person who would appreciate this approach. As I shared with a fellow passenger earlier in the trip, 'People don't care how much you know…'"

Mack finished the sentence. " 'Until they know how much you care.' Do you think you're the only one who has read Zig Ziglar?" He knew that he might get the last laugh. "Charlie, there still is the matter of our little bet."

Charlie already had the coin in the palm of his hand and studied it closely as if he'd never see it again. He'd held thousands of coins in his lifetime, but this one seemed different. The head side had Lady Liberty on it with the inscription 'E Pluribus Unum', meaning 'Out of many, one', a unifying message at the time of our country's foundation. It reminded Charlie to keep his head on straight at all times and to be proud of living in the United States. The year minted was 1889.

As he turned it over, the tail side had the national symbol, an eagle with its wings spread wide and proud. It reminded him that we need to spread our wings, try something new, and be bold in our approach. 'In God We Trust' was found above the eagle's head, evident to many but often forgotten. Charlie felt the ridges around the outside of the coin. They reminded him of the highway shoulder ridges that alert drivers before they veer completely off the road. There were plenty of times that those ridges had saved Charlie. He felt all of this significance about the coin as he handed it back to Mack.

"A bet is a bet. You were right down to the second, Mack. Congratulations! Here is your silver dollar." Charlie then handed Mack the crispest dollar bill that he had in his wallet. "Here is my dollar as well. Very nicely done."

"Charles, I will take your dollar bill as a token of your honesty in paying your bet. As I shared earlier, neither of us will go broke on a dollar, right?" Charlie nodded in agreement. Mack continued, "But I want you to have this silver dollar for three reasons."

"First of all, with it, you will have a small remembrance of our time together. You won't forget our ride, will you, Charles?" Charlie shook his head. "Whether you choose to place the coin with your other small life mementos that you've collected over the years or keep it with you in your pocket each day; that will be up to you. By the way, Charles, mementos are different than mint Mentos." Mack had to laugh at his attempted joke.

"Secondly, people today use coins to make decisions all the time. They flip to see who kicks off in overtime. Parents flip to see which child gets to sit in the car's front seat that day. Friends flip to see who buys the drinks. And as you know, Charles, much bigger decisions are made in business and in life."

"The final reason I want you to have this coin, Charles, is this: by exchanging your dollar bill with my silver dollar, we are both out nothing, yet we both have something of value. I will treasure this dollar bill as it will remind me of my friend Charles who got up and made himself vulnerable. You could have been stoned by the hothead passengers, though not likely. You could have hidden your talent under a basket and not let your light shine bright, brighter than any star in any sky on the darkest night you can imagine, but you didn't. I am blessed to call you my friend."

Charlie felt the same and the look on his face conveyed that to Mack as the two men shook hands and embraced. "Mack, I've been meaning to ask you. How long have you been conducting on the rail lines? Have you always been a conductor?"

Mack's approach to keeping it simple had Charlie's attention. "Yes, I've always been a conductor. My Father taught me many lessons, and I found the train to be a wonderful place to share them with others. I meet a great many people with each trip, station to station, situation to situation. Some, like you, seem to listen more closely than others. When I met Aura long ago, he was shaken by despair, desperate to find a new place in this world, and I was in the right place at the right time to make a difference for him."

Charlie's surprise was written all over his face, "You're talking about Aura the cab driver?"

"Yes, Charles. Aura had been through a trauma in his home country and saw things that nobody should ever have to witness. He warmed up to me as we traveled from Chicago to New Orleans. Of course, we were both much younger back then, but he's sent many a passenger to this train over the years. And when I need a cab in New Orleans, he's always there for me."

Mack continued as Charlie looked at him in amazement.

"You're probably wondering about Essie, too. She and I met on her very first trip to New Orleans. She was full of excitement and looked forward to her trip so much. I recall the look of wonder on her face, much like a young child heading to Disney for the first time. She and I have spoken many times over the years since she's one of my regulars. There are many who ride regularly, but most take the train periodically when it suits them. You, Charles, will have a choice next time you travel, and I hope you choose my way of travel. There are conductors on other routes and many passengers that you can learn from along the way. When you get back to New Orleans, here is Aura's phone number. Be sure to give him a call. He'll take you wherever you want to go."

"I can't thank you enough, Mack." Charlie was truly moved. "You have made this a most enjoyable journey. All the best to you." Charlie picked up his belongings, placed them inside his briefcase, and moved toward the doorway. As the two new friends parted, both hoped they would see each other again.

Charlie picked up his rolling bag and, one last time, he got off the sleek locomotive resting in the station. He briefly wondered if he would be transformed to 1914 in Chicago as he stepped off.

As his phone rang, Charlie walked down the platform toward the Union Station doors. It was Rita.

Chapter 17

Checking In

Charlie took Rita's call and let her know that he was on the rail platform in Chicago. It was really noisy, with the many trains idling in the background. Moving inside the station, he made his way to the marble grand stairway of the renovated Chicago Union Station, which was much quieter.

"Hey Babe, it's great to hear your voice. You will not believe it, but I had quite an adventure over the last couple of days. As I said in my text earlier, there's just too much to tell you in one sitting. It will take some time to share." Charlie paused to realize the enormity of it all. "Even a long train ride has energized me."

"You always turn challenging situations into something positive," Rita said. "You are a make – lemonade-out-of-lemons kind of guy; that you are, Charlie. Have you eaten anything?" She was always after him to eat something because he would otherwise mingle at a party or start telling a story and forget to eat. "I am sorry that I didn't text you. I have a much longer story to tell you that includes getting a new phone. Mine died, and I couldn't even get it to turn on. The Apple genius was able to get it turned on and downloaded my contacts, pictures, and texts, but the phone needed to be upgraded."

"No need to apologize. I got busy as I often do, caught up in the moment."

Rita jumped in, "Your last message said to remind you about Mack and 1914. Well?"

"Yes, I will tell you more when I see you on Friday evening. But Mack was the conductor on the train, and he and I made a special connection during the trip."

"Wasn't your grandfather a train conductor? I remember you telling me that you'd never met him. The next thing you'll say is that you met your grandfather." The phone was silent on the other end. "Charlie? Charlie? Are you there?"

"I'm here, Rita. I can't believe you remembered that." Charlie had a great-grandfather, McNulty, who worked on the East-West Burlington line but died just before Charlie was born. He'd never met him and did not have any pictures of the two of them together, but in pictures, his great-grandfather was a tall man and was often smiling. *He must have had a good sense of humor,* Charlie thought to himself. "McNulty? Mack? Nah...has to be a coincidence," he said to Rita, now thinking that maybe it wasn't so coincidental.

"What is it I'm supposed to know about 1914?" Rita asked.

"Well, I'm not sure. I got off the train three times and was transported back to life in 1914! I have a special book that I picked up several years ago. It is a business book written in 1914; it has a black leather binding and sits on the desk in my office. Will you bring it with you on Friday? You might remember that it was the basis for the book I most recently published."

"Sure, I'll bring it with me. But why?"

Charlie's stomach ached for a slab of barbequed ribs and steak fries. That free sandwich he had eaten on the train seemed so long ago. "I will tell you all about it, trust me. Babe, I have to go, my stomach is rumbling, and I will see you in just 36 hours. I'll explain it *all* on Friday."

Rita sensed that there were many things she would hear about when she picked him up. "See you Friday. Love you."

"Love you too." Charlie hung up the phone.

Charlie walked up the staircase from the Grand Hall and got his directional bearings. He turned east from Union Station and walked across the Chicago River, which was lit up with skyscraper lights. He looked up and marveled at the height of the Willis Tower while also admiring the majestic and historic Lyric Opera House right on the riverbank. Miller's Pub was just a few blocks down Adams Street toward the lakefront.

As he turned the corner onto Wabash Street, the neon sign was aglow as if welcoming him.

His mouth watered, and as he looked at the neon sign, he couldn't help but think about Tom's hardware store in Jackson and the Grand Hotel conversation with Julius and Aberdeen.

Millers was filled with customers, even after 9:00 pm. Charlie sat at the long bar and ordered a Revolution Lager. Once his meal arrived, he savored the amazing ribs and steak fries that he'd longed for on the train journey. The service from Kevin, the bartender, was excellent, and as was always the case, no doggie bag was necessary.

After paying the bill and checking out a few of the celebrity pictures on his way out, Charlie decided to walk off the meal rather than take a cab. The 8-block walk to the Hyatt was more manageable with the rolling bag by his side, and by this time, the air had cooled just a bit. He felt the energy of the Windy City streets as he had a million times before, well, more like a few hundred. He passed by a panhandler and placed a hundred-dollar bill into his Styrofoam cup. Rather than asking when he ate last, he simply said, "God bless you."

Charlie was satisfied that he had made new friends like Jackson and Jessica, who had already connected on LinkedIn. He knew that the $100 bill he'd given to Simon the drifter may have bought him several meals, or maybe a few bottles of whiskey. Either way, Charlie knew that he was a richer man, having a nice shiny silver dollar coin in his pocket.

In addition to the registration desk, the second floor at the Hyatt was also home to one of the most intriguing lobby bars in Chicago. The bar had multi-story glass windows, and its circular top-shelf bar seemed to be calling him, but so did a comfortable bed and a good night's sleep. He chose to complete his check-in and take the elevator to the 15th floor.

Once settled into his suite, Charlie received a text from the manager, who was making sure that his accommodation was first class.

Charlie texted back that the champagne was a nice touch and that he'd share more about Champaign when the manager stopped at the book signing on Thursday. Charlie thought about how much customer service meant to him and how some people weren't as responsive as they'd been in the past. He believed that those who went over and above would always win and that an effective approach to responsiveness was bound to be successful.

Charlie called Sarge, knowing that his old friend was up at all hours of the night anyway. "Hey buddy, are we still on for the York Tavern on Friday afternoon? You won't believe it, but I took the train to Chicago from New Orleans rather than flying into O'Hare. I would have called to let you know, but it wouldn't have made much difference. Today was intended to be an off day for me before going downtown for my book signing tomorrow."

"You took the train from New Orleans? Come on now!" Sarge and Charlie had been friends since fifth grade. Sarge had retired and worked hard to keep up his relationship with Charlie. He drove his Harley to Cincinnati occasionally. He was a massive Skyline Chili fan and ate it as often as possible. "I got about a dozen of the guys coming to The York at about noon on Friday! Want me to pick you up for an early breakfast at Lou Mitchells? We could hang out at the Planetarium and maybe drive down Lake Shore Drive." Charlie thought that it would be fun but had an alternate plan.

"Nah, that's okay, I'll grab a Metra train from Union Station to Hinsdale. You never know who you'll meet on a train, which will make for another adventure. It'll work out perfectly if you can pick me up there. Rita will meet us at The York, and afterward, we're heading to Summerfest in Milwaukee. You are welcome to join us if you want to. Summerfest may have a fried grouper sandwich." Charlie knew how to push Sarge's buttons and knew that he wouldn't likely come.

"I'll let you know on Friday. See you then, buddy." Charlie hung up and plugged his phone into the charger on the nightstand lamp.

The city's lights glimmered into Charlie's room as they had each time he stayed downtown, especially with the view along the Chicago River. The Tribune Tower and Wrigley building had matching blue lights on top, which always made Charlie feel at home. He recalled a snowy April when he and Rita celebrated her birthday, her first real trip to Chicago with Charlie as her guide. He loved the cityscape at night and always slept like a baby when he was there. Putting his head on the pillow, Charlie knew that even if God gave him another 30 hours, he'd still only sleep six.

AFTERWORD

Connections

The thought of adventure travel began when I was just a child. We didn't have much money back then, and growing up in the Chicago area, my adventures took me to Wrigley Field, Comiskey Park, and other places in the Midwest. Eventually, I would travel with my parents separately (they divorced when I was only 7 years old), but it was not exotic travel. As a business professional and with my family, I've traveled all over this amazing country!

--- ### ---

Some questions you may have after your reading:

Yes, my maternal great-grandfather (George McNulty...aka Mack) really was a conductor on the Burlington-Northern train line, which ran from Chicago to Los Angeles. However, he passed away before I was born in 1962. He and my great-grandmother lived in Chicago for most of their lives, and he would have been working for the railroad in 1914. He was born in 1889, which is why I chose that year for Mack's Morgan silver dollar coin.

My paternal great-grandfather (Karl Moravec) likely was an alcoholic, moving from place to place, doing odd jobs on the near west side of Chicago. My great-grandmother (his wife Anna) died in June of 1915. Shortly after that, his two children were placed in an orphanage at the ages of 11 and 13; this was my grandfather (Charlie) and his older sister, my great-aunt Mary. These events certainly shaped each of their lives. My Grandpa Moravec started working at a very young age as a delivery errand boy, working his way up to become a salesman in the south & west suburbs of Chicago. He sold caskets for a living and was revered by his funeral home clients. I know this because I have talked with several of them, including the one who hosted his funeral visitation, where I delivered his eulogy in 1991. Many of my extended family members have said I naturally came by my salesmanship from him; he never met a stranger that he couldn't talk with.

By my account, the Amtrak train system continues to build customer confidence by combatting its challenges around on-time performance. Based on what I've researched, much of it has to do with sharing the rails with freight operators who control the traffic flow. Amtrak is constantly working with freight line companies; they are finding some success and moving the needle. My tale of unexpected connections is a fictionalized *exaggeration* from a train timeline perspective, which allows me, as a writer, some creative play with the timeline of events; delays of six hours or more are rare, even on cross-country trips.

As far as I know, Amtrak has never served champagne in Champaign. That said, their customer service level is impressive, and in my opinion, their leadership team is doing a fantastic job at making train travel attractive. A special thanks go out to the customer care team at the New Orleans Union Passenger Terminal (Danielle, Pam, and Tony), who provided me with an amazing send-off on my most recent train trip to Chicago. Wren was my train attendant on the City of New Orleans train, and along with the team of conductors on board, they made my long-distance experience a memorable one.

Airline travel today is challenging at best but given our need/desire to be somewhere fast, flying is still the most economical and timely option. Many people my age or older say things like: "Do you remember when they served full hot meals on planes? Remember when you could go to the airport and simply walk through the terminals to watch planes take off and land? Remember when we didn't have to wait in long lines through TSA or have the kind of delays that we have today?" All of them are true, and while 9-11 had much to do with the changes, society has demanded more: more destinations, more travel time options, and more airports. In 1980 there were 4,814 public airports; as of reporting in 2022, there are now 5,193. The train option does have many amenities and comforts, despite the time of travel, and I personally will compare the choices each time I travel from now on.

Racial and sexual biases still exist today, and in 1914, the United States was nearly 50 years removed from the end of the Civil War, a point I've made several times in my book. If we went back to 2014, 1964, 1864, or even further, it would be easy to find example after example at all levels of society. I feel we need to encourage diversity, equity, and inclusion conversations, not only with discussion and rhetoric but also with definitive actions that get ALL of us interacting personally and professionally on a daily basis.

In June 1914, WWI was about to explode in Europe; shortly thereafter, the U.S. got involved. Innovation from the industrial age was taking place, and our country was becoming much more mobile with the number of vehicles available through mass production capabilities. I am fascinated by history and hope that you, the reader, can explore a historical period that intrigues you. Books abound on historical fiction and non-fiction that stand the test of time.

If you haven't found a single "take-away" from the book, you haven't looked closely enough. Oftentimes, written business fables are prescribed with lessons that include bullet points and chapter summaries and have accompanying study guides. Echoes Across the Tracks really is intended to meander from topic to topic, idea to idea, connected by the rails and the surroundings.

Short Sleepers Syndrome as it is commonly known is a much lesser known and studied sleep disorder that affects a very small portion of the population. The researchers at the University of California, San Francisco continue to effort more detailed information as do other sleep experts. I'm not a sleep doctor, nor do I play one on T.V. I just know that my body doesn't need as much sleep as many others and that the information I have points me in this direction.

www.ucsf.edu/news/2019/08/415261/after-10-year-search-scientists-find-second-short-sleep-gene

The final connecting point to 1914-1915 is the book *Modern Marketing Methods and Salesmanship* which was published in 1914. It is long out of print and the book reads like a King James Bible due to its use of language about sales that we don't use today. If you are interested in the book that was being sold at the Convention Center in New Orleans at the beginning of my story, you'll have to wait until it comes out in print...it is my current work in progress. You can reach me with feedback (positive or negative) about the book through my LinkedIn profile, social media, email, or snail mail.

CHAMBERS OF COMMERCE

The world of chambers of commerce is a magnificent orchestration of community with players that include Executive Directors and Chamber Boards, Economic Development Councils, Convention & Visitors Bureaus, and Government bodies (City, Town, Township, County, Regional, State). These entities meld together with area businesses, non-profit organizations, and area schools (in most instances) to create an environment for cooperation and success in a specified geographic area.

I have been blessed with a late-in-life career change with the Colerain Chamber of Commerce in suburban Cincinnati. We have accomplished a great deal in just our first 10 years of existence and my first four years, which began just as COVID hit Cincinnati in mid-March 2020. Since then, I have met and collaborated with over 100 chambers of commerce in Ohio and across the U.S., including those along the rail lines between New Orleans and Chicago.

Chambers are vital to many communities because they provide strategic planning, marketing opportunities, awards ceremonies, networking events, and ancillary benefits to many smaller businesses that might not otherwise have access to them. They also connect those businesses with larger organizations in their area to create a credible community that cross-pollinates ideas that benefit everyone concerned.

If you or your business have not looked into your local chamber of commerce, I suggest that you do so right away. Additional resources are available through statewide chambers of commerce and the Association of Chamber of Commerce Executives (ACCE), which provides access to complex data (in easy-to-read format). There are many professional development resources to help small business owners with some of the challenges identified in my story. Succession and strategic planning are as vital today as they have ever been, and I recommend talking through options every day.

Made in the USA
Columbia, SC
04 May 2024

7e46ebee-4f4b-4f59-84b1-42d151291213R01